HISTORICAL SITES IN ISRAEL

by MOSHE PEARLMAN and YAACOV YANNAI

FOREWORD BY
YIGAEL YADIN
PROFESSOR OF ARCHAEOLOGY AT THE
HEBREW UNIVERSITY, JERUSALEM

THE VANGUARD PRESS · NEW-YORK

THIRD PRINTING 1965

© 1964 and 1965 by M. Pearlman and Y. Yannai

Lay-out Zur—Avnon

PRINTED IN ISRAEL FOR VANGUARD PRESS, N.Y.
PELI-P.E.C. PRINTING WORKS LTD., RAMAT GAN

CONTENTS

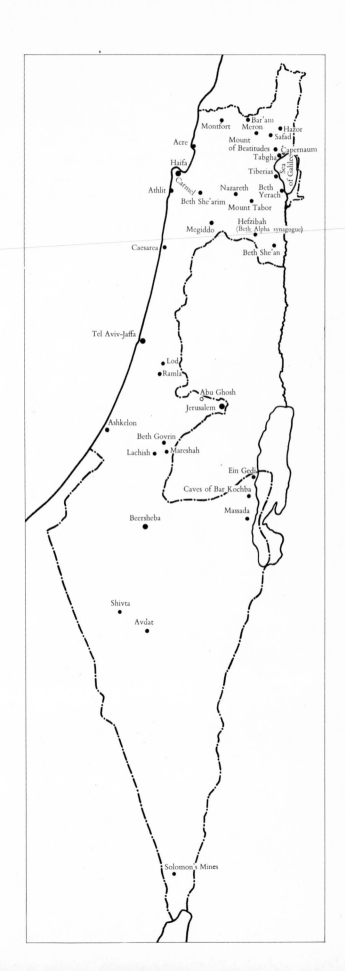

AUTHORS' NOTE

It is the purpose of this book to present, in non-technical language, a brief historical background to the most important sites of antiquity in Israel. Wherever relevant, the material is based on the latest archaeological discoveries.

Israel, with its rich past, abounds in ancient places. Not all have been included in these pages. In our selection of sites, we have been guided broadly by three criteria: importance — as the location of historic events, as the subject of significant archaeological excavation, or as the site of well-preserved ruins; accessibility (except for Massada and The Caves of Bar Kochba, which were too important to omit and which, in any case, will become more easily accessible in the near future); and beauty of surroundings. Most of them, indeed, are among the country's beauty spots.

The sites are presented roughly in their geographic order from north to south. We have, however, led off with Jerusalem because of its special place in history.

This book is intended for the general reader. Those with a more specialised interest in the history and archaeology of a particular site are referred to the bibliography at the end. We have also included a detailed chronological table.

We are indebted to Dr. Avraham Negev, of the Hebrew University's Archaeological Department, for going over the proofs and making valuable suggestions.

M. P.
Y. Y.

Jerusalem, 1964

FOREWORD

There has long been the need for a book on the important ancient sites in Israel which is readable, which incorporates the latest archaeological discoveries, and which is scientifically accurate yet unburdened by the kind of minute detail which can be of interest only to the specialist. HISTORICAL SITES IN ISRAEL fills this need.

The intelligent visitor to Israel's antiquities often seeks more than the brief descriptions which appear in many guide books. On the other hand he can find little aid from the technical works which are inevitably crowded with scientific detail and are for the most part written in dry academic language. On one site alone he may have to work through several volumes.

HISTORICAL SITES IN ISRAEL covers all the important sites within a single volume, presents all the salient facts which a visitor would wish to know, introduces him to the adventure of archaeology "without tears", and heightens the intellectual enjoyment of his visit. The writing is impressive, and so is the rich selection of the numerous illustrations. It is a book that may be enjoyed equally by the visitor to Israel and by the armchair reader.

Several factors have contributed to the success of this book. The authors show an admirable understanding of the needs of the reader and have had the skill to present in word and picture exactly what he requires. Both have an intimate familiarity with the country. And both are close to the scientific sources and to the archaeological work undertaken in Israel.

Moshe Pearlman, resuming his writing career after distinguished service in the Ministry for Foreign Affairs and in the Prime Minister's Office, is the author of several important books on Israel and its problems. He also wrote the popular booklets on those sites of antiquity which have been restored, working closely with the archaeologists who carried out the excavations.

Yaacov Yannai is the Commissioner for Landscaping and the Preservation of Historic Sites in Israel, attached to the Prime Minister's Office. It is he who has been responsible for the remarkable restoration of many archaeological sites in the country, notably Caesarea, Beth She'arim, Avdat, Shivta, Bar'am and Beth Alpha, which are among those dealt with in the book.

HISTORICAL SITES IN ISRAEL is a handsome addition to the literature on this ancient land. It is a valuable book which will be read with profit and pleasure by visitor and stay-at-home alike.

YIGAEL YADIN

JERUSALEM

Jerusalem, perched high amid the Judean hills, has been more familiar to more people than any other place on earth. It lies 2700 feet above sea level and is 44 miles inland from Tel Aviv on the Mediterranean coast. Its origins reach back to the mists of antiquity, but it is believed to have started its tumultuous history, packed with incident and ideas which have shaped the behaviour of half the human race, at some time during the 4th millennium B.C. The impact of this history is very real to all who have been touched by the Bible. This is the city of David and Solomon and Hezekiah, of Isaiah and Jeremiah, of Haggai, Malachi, Habakkuk and Zechariah, of Ezra and Nehemiah, of Judah the Maccabee and the Hasmonian dynasty. This is the city of Jesus' last ministry and the place where He was crucified. Moslems, too, hold Jerusalem holy — after Mecca and Medina — as the city from which Mohammed is believed to have ascended to heaven.

The renown of Jerusalem reflects the triumph of the spirit over the transient fabric of the material world. Jerusalem was blessed with neither special economic nor strategic favours which might explain why it should ever have become more than a small, anonymous, mountain village with a fate different from that of most contemporary villages which have long vanished. Its height gave it some military advantage. Natural springs gave it a moderate source of water. It enjoyed a most equable climate. These were sufficient to make it a feasible site of early settlement, but not to give it importance. It was off the main caravan routes, and it held no strategic key to the conquest of vast areas prized by the ancient warring empires. No. Its importance is the product of the cultural giants of old, the philosopher kings and the Biblical prophets, who made Jerusalem their centre. Amid its rugged landscape, breathing the pure mountain air, they gave their wisdom to the world — and changed it. As Isaiah proclaimed: "For out of Zion shall go forth the law, and the word of the Lord from Jerusalem."

Jerusalem is the Hebrew for "City of Peace". In the days of Abraham — about the 18th Century B.C. — we learn from Genesis that it was known as Salem. It

is also mentioned in Egyptian documents of that period. When Joshua reached the country in the 13th Century, Jerusalem was a fortified city held by the Jebusites — and held strongly. No conquest was attempted then. Not, indeed, until the successful assault of David, at the beginning of the 10th Century B.C., did it become an Israelite city. Its history of importance dates from that moment. Thereafter it is referred to in the Bible also as Zion and as the City of David. It was David who developed Jerusalem, built up its fortifications, erected sumptuous public buildings, made it the permanent site of the Ark of the Covenant and planned to construct a Temple to the Lord. It was David who proclaimed Jerusalem the capital of Israel. It has remained, from that time, the eternal spiritual capital of the Jewish people. Over the next thousand years, it was to be also, for varying periods, the political capital of Israel, or, after the monarchy was divided, of Judah. Then came a gap of nineteen centuries. In our own day, after Israel's independence in 1948, it has become once again the capital of the country.

King Solomon added magnificence to the work started by his father. He enlarged the city and launched a remarkable building programme, crowned by the construction of the Temple which David had hoped to build. It was dedicated about the year 953 B.C. From the Biblical account, the Temple was certainly the most impressive building in the land, fashioned from the finest materials obtainable in the Middle East, and every architectural detail reflected the exquisite workmanship of master craftsmen. The ornamental decorations were the inspiration of the leading artists. This we know from the written texts alone, not from the physical remains. For this Temple was destroyed in 587 B.C. by the Babylonian king Nebuchadnezzar.

Not satisfied with this destruction, Nebuchadnezzar sought to wipe out all prospect of Jerusalem's ever again becoming the centre of Jewish life — and of possible further rebellion — by carrying off most of its Jews to Babylon. It was from there, "by the waters of Babylon", that the cry was uttered which echoed through all the centuries of Jewish history:

"We hanged our harps upon the willows in the midst thereof
For there they that carried us away captive required of us a song;
And they that spoiled us required of us mirth,
Saying, Sing us one of the songs of Zion.

How shall we sing the Lord's song in a strange land?
If I forget thee, O Jerusalem, let my right hand forget her cunning.
If I do not remember thee, let my tongue cleave to the roof of my mouth;
If I prefer not Jerusalem above my chief joy." (Psalms 137)

13

Less than fifty years later, however, the great Babylonian empire fell as suddenly as it had arisen, overwhelmed by Cyrus, founder of a new Persian empire. In the nature of things, Cyrus was inclined to deal kindly with the victims of the enemy he had just vanquished — among them the Jewish exiles. And their monotheism was a concept which could appeal to a follower of the idealistic Persian religion. Within a few months of his victory in 538 B.C., he allowed the Jews to return to Jerusalem and there to rebuild their Temple. This Second Temple was completed in the year 516 B.C. It lasted until the Roman destruction in 70 A.D.

For some two hundred years after the return of the Babylonian exiles, Jerusalem was once again the centre of Jewish life in the country — now part of the Persian empire. It was considerably strengthened in the middle of the 5th Century by the inspired leadership of Ezra the Scribe and Nehemiah, a distinguished Jewish administrator who was close to the Persian throne.

In 332 B.C., the Persian empire collapsed, conquered by Alexander the Great. He left Jerusalem untouched, but with his death came a disintegration of his dominion, his generals rivalling each other for control. One of them, Ptolemy, who had taken Egypt, invaded the land, and for the next 120 years Jerusalem came under the authority of his dynasty. It was a benevolent rule, the Ptolemies allowing the Jews almost complete autonomy; but in 198 B.C., the country was wrested from Egyptian control by the Seleucids of Syria, descendants of another of Alexander's generals, Seleucus, who had set up his capital in Antioch.

Serious trouble befell the Jews of Jerusalem when the Seleucid king Antiochus ascended the throne in 175 B.C., assuming the megalomanic title Epiphanes. (The ordinary meaning of this Greek word is "Illustrious"; but it is also an abbreviation of the expression for "God-manifest", and this was the meaning intended by Antiochus, as is clear from the symbols on the coins he had struck.) Born in Athens and idolising Greek ways, Antiochus Epiphanes sought passionately to Hellenize the provinces of his empire, to impose a standard pattern of life upon his heterogeneous vassals, to permit no separatism, and to compel all to worship Greek gods. The Jewish religion was to be abolished.

In Jerusalem, the holy Temple was defiled. Within its sacred precincts, Greek troops practised heathen rites, introduced the image of a Greek deity, sacrificed swine on the altar, destroyed the Scrolls of the Law. The observance of the Jewish religion was made punishable by death. So was failure to respect the new customs. Jews were butchered for refusing to eat pig's flesh or to bow down to Greek images.

In 167 B.C. the Jews revolted. They were led by the family of a priest of the House of Hasmon named Mattathias, and his son, Judah, known as the Maccabee. Starting as a guerrilla force, operating from mountain fastnesses, the Hasmoneans, or Maccabees, as they also came to be called, eventually developed into a national

liberation army which drove out the conqueror and restored Jewish independence. Their first act was to cleanse the Temple and re-fortify and rebuild Jerusalem. The Hasmonean kingdom lasted until 63 B.C. when Jerusalem fell to the Romans.

In the year 37 B.C., Herod, grandson of an Idumaean Jewish convert, reached the throne as a vassal of Rome. Though cruel and self-seeking, and spurned by most of the Jews as a renegade who fawned on imperial Rome, Herod was a brilliant organiser and administrator, a man with a colossal drive to build. He even built a huge city — Caesarea — whose remains may be seen today. He also left his mark on Jerusalem, raising a palace and public buildings, and, above all, reconstructing the Temple. It had remained virtually unaltered for almost five hundred years. Indeed, the sole relic of the Temple still standing today is one of the walls restored by Herod. This is the celebrated Wailing Wall, in the Old City, on the Jordan side of the border, to which no Jew is now allowed access. (The Wailing Wall is so called because some two hundred years later, the Roman ban on Jewish entry into the city was gradually relaxed to permit Jews once a year "to wail over its stones").

It was during Herod s reign that a Child was born in Bethlehem, and grew to manhood in Nazareth. It was shortly after Herod's death that the Roman Procurator of Judea, Pontius Pilate, ordered the crucifixion in Jerusalem of this Galilean Jew, Jesus of Nazareth, little dreaming of the effect upon mankind his action was to have.

In 66 A.D. came the great revolt of the Jews against the Romans. Jerusalem was the seat and stronghold of the Jewish patriot forces. They must have known how frail were their chances, but they were determined to go down fighting. They held out four years. In 70 A.D., the city fell to Titus, son of the famous Roman general Vespasian and himself a redoubtable soldier. The Temple went up in flames and thousands of Jews were slaughtered or carried off into captivity. A few managed to escape to carry on the struggle from Massada.

For a fleeting moment in history some 60 years later, Jerusalem again enjoyed Jewish sovereignty. This came during the Bar Kochba revolt, 132–135 A.D., when his zealots managed to drive the Romans from the city. They even started preparations to restore the Temple, but they had too little time. The Romans, realising the gravity of the rebellion, brought up the full might of their military machine, and once again Jerusalem fell.

This time, by order of the emperor Hadrian, the city of Jerusalem was razed and a new, heathen city erected on its ruins. As part of the policy of suppressing Jewry, the name of the country was changed from Judea to Syria Palestina — hence Palestine — and the city on the site of Jerusalem was called Aelia Capitolina. Here the Romans built a forum, a shrine to Aphrodite, a theatre, a circus and the

Head of figurine of Astarte found at Ramat Rachel.

inevitable baths. On the ruins of the Temple they built a temple to Jupiter Capitolinus. (From this came the new name of the city. Aelia was taken from Hadrian's family name.) An edict went out from Hadrian prohibiting any Jew from setting foot within this city, on pain of death. Incidentally, Aelia Capitolina excluded Mount Zion. Thus, for the first time, this historic hill was outside the city walls.

At the beginning of the 4th Century A.D., the emperor Constantine (306–337), the first emperor to accept Christianity as his personal faith, built the church of the Holy Sepulchre in Jerusalem (the site is thought to have been that of the Roman shrine to Aphrodite). Later in the century, with the splitting of the Roman empire into eastern and western parts, Palestine came within the eastern — the Byzantine — division. During the Byzantine period, Jerusalem became the main site for basilicas and monasteries.

More than one thousand years after Cyrus, the Persians again conquered Jerusalem, driving out the Byzantines in 614 A.D. But only for a brief period. It was retaken by Byzantium in 627, to be lost ten years later to Moslem assault. Then came the rule of Islamic Caliphs for several centuries, and during this period a number of mosques were erected, mostly on sites already hallowed by Jewish and Christian shrines. The most famous Moslem sanctuary built at this time (end of the 7th Century A.D.), the Haram ash-Sharif, with its twin shrines of the Dome of the Rock and the Mosque of Aksa, was erected on the original grounds of Solomon's Temple.

In 1099 A.D., Jerusalem fell to the Crusaders, who promptly carried out a vast slaughter of both Moslems and Jews. In the year 1100, Crusader Baldwin was crowned King of Jerusalem. 87 years later, it was reconquered by the Saracens under the celebrated Saladin. From then on, scattered Jewish communities from many parts of the world resumed the pilgrimage to the holy city. (The visit of the great thinker Maimonides, in 1267, gave much encouragement to the Jewish inhabitants of Jerusalem.)

In the 13th Century, the eternal city again changed hands several times. Conquered by the Egyptians, who destroyed the Crusader fortifications, it was re-taken by the Saracens under Saladin's grandson, destroyed in turn by the Mongols in 1260, and rebuilt by the Mameluke sultan Baibars.

In 1517 came the Turkish conquest, and Jerusalem was refortified by the sultan Suleiman. The walls that he built, completed in 1538, are those which may be seen today encircling the Old City. They are very well preserved. They, too, exclude Mount Zion — which is part of Jewish Jerusalem — for they were built on the foundations of the walls of Aelia Capitolina.

The Old City and its Holy Places lie within the kingdom of Jordan. The city to the west of the Turkish walls is the Jerusalem of Israel today.

Such was the stormy history of ancient Jerusalem, a history of war and peace, of splendour and squalor, of lofty wisdom and of blood flowing in its gutters. The story of the Jews and Jerusalem is repeatedly interrupted by a succession of conquerors — Egyptians, Assyrians, Babylonians, Persians, Ptolemies, Seleucids, Romans, Moslem Arabs, Seljuks, Fatimids, Crusaders, Saracens, Mongols, Mamelukes, Ottomans. Yet throughout the three thousand years since David made it· the capital, the attachment of the Jews to Jerusalem has remained unbroken. It is a unique attachment. Through all the centuries of their dispersion, in whatever far corner of the earth they have found themselves, the Jews have prayed for the return to Zion. Their synagogues, in whatever part of the world they have been built, have always been designed with the Ark of the Law oriented towards Jerusalem. History has no parallel to this mystic bond. Without it, there would be no State of Israel today.

Of Jerusalem's sites of antiquity, the most venerable and, for Jews, the most sacred in all Israel is Mount Zion, the traditional site of king David's sepulchre. "So David slept with his fathers, and was buried in the city of David." (I Kings II, 10). Mount Zion is also the nearest point to the most important relic still standing of the original Temple — the Wailing Wall.

For Christians, Mount Zion is sacred as the place both where the Last Supper was conducted, and where Mary fell into eternal sleep.

The chamber which has become known as the tomb of David is reached through the ground-floor court and halls of a mediaeval structure. It was revealed during the erection on this spot of a Crusader church in the 12th Century A.D. The second storey of this building contains the Coenaculum, believed to be the "upper room" mentioned in the New Testament where Jesus and his disciples celebrated the first night of the Jewish Festival of Passover, an event known ever since as the "Last Supper". "His disciples said unto him, where wilt thou that we go and prepare that thou mayest eat the passover? And he sendeth forth two of his disciples, and saith unto them, Go ye into the city, and there shall meet you a man bearing a pitcher of water: follow him. And wheresoever he shall go in, say ye to the goodman of the house, The Master saith, Where is the guestchamber, where I shall eat the passover with my disciples? And he will shew you a large upper room furnished and prepared: there make ready for us." (Mark XIV, 12–15). The Coenaculum — from the Latin for "refectory" — was rebuilt in the Gothic style by Franciscan monks in the 14th Century, after the Crusader church on this site had been destroyed by the Saracens. This is the Gothic hall that may be seen today, its pointed arches springing from the large pillars that rise from the ground-floor hall that leads to David's tomb. The earliest Christian building erected on this site was the Byzantine Hagia Zion, known as the Mother of Churches.

The rock-cut tombs of Sanhedria, 1st Century A.D.

Adjoining this building, with its precious associations for Jews and Christians, and also part of the original Hagia compound, are the rotunda of the Church of the Dormition and the Dormition Monastery. The cupola and the towering belfry dominate Mount Zion and are the most familiar landmarks in Jerusalem. The belfry still bears deep scars from Arab shells and machine-gun fire during the war of 1948. The Dormition buildings are new, having been built by the Benedictine Fathers in 1906, but the ground they cover has an ancient history. According to Christian tradition this is where Mary died, the place of *Dormitio Sanctae Mariae* — the Sleep of Saint Mary. At the edge of the decorated floor beneath the dome of the circular church are steps which lead down to the crypt, and in the centre is a reclining statue of Mary on her death bed.

The valley which stretches eastward from the foot of Mount Zion is the source of a word which has been adopted by the English language as a synonym for "hell". This is the Valley of the son of Hinnom, believed to have been the scene of child-sacrifices in ancient times. Valley of Hinnom in Hebrew is "Gei Hinnom", of which "Gehenna" is a Greek corruption.

A few yards to the southeast of the modern King David Hotel is the 1st Century B.C. tomb built by king Herod for his family. (He himself was buried in a hill near Bethlehem, three miles away.) This tomb, whose location is mentioned by Josephus, was discovered towards the end of the last century. It has been cleared in recent years. Entrance is through a sunken court and a short tunnel, hewn out of the rock, which was originally blocked by a beautifully preserved "rolling stone". The tunnel leads into a hall and corridor in which there are openings to the burial chambers. At the time of the discovery of this ancient mausoleum three stone coffins were found, one of them decorated with a flowered relief. They were removed during the second world war and are now in St. Constantine's Monastery in the Old City.

Almost as ancient as this is the necropolis of Sanhedria, at the northern edge of the city. Here are the rock-cut burial caves, dating back to the 1st Century A.D., of the patrician Jewish families of Jerusalem. The largest and most ornate of these tombs is considered by popular tradition to have been the communal resting place of the judges of Israel's Supreme Court in olden times, the Sanhedrin. This has given the name — Sanhedria — to the burial area and indeed to this quarter of Jerusalem. The seventy-one members of the Sanhedrin were drawn from the greatest sages of the period.

This tomb is a huge, three-storeyed, artificial cave with several burial chambers. The most spectacular is the first to be reached from the entrance. Cut in its north wall are two storeys of vertical, arched burial niches. The lower row of seven have been cut directly into the face of the wall. The upper row of six, however, have been set back, cut in the rear walls of three wide vaulted cavities, so that each

cavity contains two burial niches. Openings in this main hall lead to other burial chambers, and there are also steps which descend to the tombs below ground level. This Sanhedrin cave is approached through a large forecourt and a handsome stone entrance, topped by an elaborate pediment decorated with reliefs of pomegranates and acanthus leaves.

But possibly the oldest burial cave in Jerusalem is one situated in the heart of Rehavia, one of the more elegant residential districts of the new city. It was found by accident only a few years ago. In 1956, while excavating a site for the foundations of a new house in Alfasi Street — it would have been No. 10 — the labourers suddenly found their picks going through the roof of a cave. Israel builders, always alert to the prospect of turning up some ancient relic in this historic land, know exactly what to do under such circumstances. They stop work and quickly contact the Government Department of Antiquities. That is what the labourers at 10 Alfasi Street did. Archaeologists who came rushing over were delighted to conduct a scientific clearance of the cave. (The prospective new house-owner was less delighted). The result of their study showed this to have been a burial cave dating back to the 2nd Century B.C., during the Hasmonean period. A rock-cut passage led to chambers with burial niches in the walls. The entrance hall contains primitive wall-drawings, among them a curious one of a sea-battle. An Aramaic inscription on one wall mentions the name "Jason", apparently the principal person to be buried here. This cave is therefore now known as Jason's Tomb.

A few hundred yards to the west of this tomb is an ancient monastery, built at the foot of a slope which is covered by old olive trees. This is the Monastery of the Cross, and the vale in which it lies is called the Valley of the Cross. The name springs from the legend that it was a tree in this valley which provided the timber for the cross on which Jesus was crucified.

The building is a fortified mediaeval monastery which is believed to rest in part on Roman foundations. Its stout walls are heavily buttressed and only the silver dome and the belfry suggest from the outside that it is a Crusader shrine. Entry is through a small chin-high porch in the east wall which opens on to an inner court. Above the court are arrayed a complex system of staircases and terraces which serve the sundry chambers built against each of the fortress walls. A short arcade running off the far corner of the court leads to the church. This is a fine 12th Century Crusader basilica, modest in size but with beautifully vaulted ceilings and a high dome above the altar. Original mosaics cover sections of the floor of the nave. Parts of the walls of fortress and basilica are restorations. The Monastery of the Cross now belongs to the Greek Orthodox Church.

On the high ground to the west of the valley rise the monumental new buildings of the capital. Immediately above the monastery is the compound of the National

Entrance to king Herod's family tomb, built in 1st Century B.C.

Decorated capital from royal Judean citadel unearthed at Ramat Rachel.

Museum of Art and Archaeology. Adjoining it is the Shrine of the Book which houses the Dead Sea Scrolls and the recently discovered letters of Bar Kochba.

Three quarters of a mile to the south of Mount Zion is a wooded ridge known as the Hill of Evil Counsel. The handsome building on the summit was formerly the residence of the High Commissioner during the years of the British Mandate (1922–1948), and is now the headquarters of the United Nations Truce Supervision Organisation. It was natural for the politically minded population of the country to consider the site well and appropriately named — in a contemporary context. But its origin goes back some two thousand years to an ancient piece of "evil counsel". The reference is to Caiaphas, the priest, in the 1st Century, who had a summer house on this spot. It was here that he is believed to have given the kind of counsel which led to the arrest of Jesus. (Some hold that this took place at Dir Abu Tor, the low mound to the immediate north).

The next ridge to the south, and indeed the southernmost ridge in Jerusalem, is Ramat Rachel, site of a kibbutz and also of an observation platform from which there is an excellent view of the city and the surrounding countryside, including Bethlehem across the border. In 1958, a five-season archaeological dig was started here under the direction of Dr. Yohanan Aharoni.

The most important discovery were the remains of a royal Judean citadel dating back to the end of the 7th and beginning of the 6th Century B.C., shortly before the destruction of the First Temple. They were found early on in the excavations, and were thought at first to have been the work, in the 8th Century, of king Uzziah, whose prolific building activities are given special mention in the Bible. Later, however, Aharoni dug up the stamp of a seal of the steward of king Jehoiakim, who reigned in Judah from 609–598 B.C. It is Dr. Aharoni's theory that since Jehoiakim's tenure of the throne may have been somewhat shaky, ruling as he did with the political support of pharaoh Necho of Egypt, he probably thought it prudent to build himself a stronghold in the suburbs of Jerusalem.

The small inner citadel, built on the high ground, was fortified by a casemate wall constructed of hewn stone. In it were the remains of handsome buildings, with fine masonry and decorated capitals similar to those found in the royal palaces excavated at Samaria and Megiddo. In the final season, the archaeologists found remains of a large outer wall, built of unhewn stones to an average thickness of ten feet. This was a solid wall, apparently of the "salients and recesses" type.

One of the upper strata of the Ramat Rachel excavations showed that this settlement was rebuilt by the Jewish exiles who returned after the Persian conquest of Babylonia when Judah became a province of the Persian empire. Many jar handles belonging to this period were found stamped with the letters YHD — denoting "Yehud", the Aramaic name of Judah — and YRShLM — Jerusalem.

Also found were seal-impressions bearing the hitherto unknown names of Jewish governors of Judah under Persian rule, such as "Yehoazar" and "Ahiyahu."

One of the earlier Judean relics was found in a cave, with tiers of niches cut in the rock, belonging to a period of settlement several centuries later. The relic was a stone capital which had been brought into the cave and apparently set up as an altar. A bowl had been scooped out of one of its surfaces, no doubt to serve some libation ritual.

Altogether, seven levels of settlement were uncovered on this site, ranging from the 7th Century B.C. to the 7th Century A.D. The royal citadel, destroyed by the Babylonian king Nebuchadnezzar in the final days of the First Temple, was replaced by a new citadel built by the returning Jewish exiles. It lasted until the 3rd Century B.C. The next level of settlement continued well into the Roman period, but was destroyed with the destruction of the Second Temple. In the 2nd or 3rd Century A.D., the site was occupied by the Roman Tenth Legion. Of the buildings they erected, there are remains of a bath-house and a palatial dwelling with a colonnaded court. Many of the floors of the buildings bear the seal of this legion. In the 5th Century A.D., under Byzantium, a church and monastery were built, and among the relics found in the monastery compound were remains of large storage vessels, an oil press and water cisterns. The topmost stratum — the last level of habitation — contained ruins of a primitive settlement belonging to the early Arabic period. Their buildings, of poor standard, were built on the remains of the Byzantine structures.

The excavation area adjoins the observation platform and is open to view.

Four miles westwards from the centre of the city lies Jerusalem's most charming suburb — Ein Karem. It looks like a mediaeval Judean hamlet clinging to the hill-side, its stone buildings framed by slender cypresses that stand decorative guard upon the terraces. Ein Karem is a sight of beauty at all times; but it is best seen when the sun is low and the shadows are long.

Historically, the interest of Ein Karem lies in its association with St. John the Baptist, for this is the traditional place of his birth. It is also believed to be the place where Mary visited his mother, the "city of Juda" to which Mary made her way when, after the Annunciation, she "arose in those days and went into the hill country. . . And entered into the house of Zacharias, and saluted Elizabeth." (Luke I, 39–40). Elizabeth, cousin to Mary, was with child at the time, even though she and her husband, Zacharias, a Jewish priest, were advanced in years. They named the baby John. This was the John who spent his early years in the wilderness, wandering "into all the country about Jordan, preaching the baptism of repentance for the remission of sins". (Luke III, 3).

It is understandable, therefore, that, in the early days of Christianity, two special sites in Ein Karem, the birth-place and the visit, should have been

commemorated by religious buildings. The tradition was continued in later periods.

Over the traditional birth-place now stands the Franciscan Church and Monastery of St. John. This is just off the main road, close to the entrance to Ein Karem. It is a 17th Century structure, built on the ruins of earlier churches. Steps to the left of the altar lead down to the Birth Grotto of the Baptist. This is a cave with marble reliefs round the walls depicting scenes from the life of St. John as recounted in the Gospel. It is an ancient cave but less so are the marble reliefs, which are reflective of the period of the artist rather than that of the subject. Much older decorations are the Roman, Byzantine and Crusader mosaics, remains of churches of those periods, which are preserved in the basement of the present basilica. One of them, a 5th-6th Century A.D. mosaic with the familiar motif of birds and plants, has in the centre a Greek inscription: "Hail, ye martyrs of the Lord."

On the other side of the village, built against the slope of the hill, is the second Roman Catholic shrine in Ein Karem. This is the Franciscan Church of the Visitation. It is a modern two storey building — a very fine one — constructed only a few years ago on the ruins of a Crusader church. The site is believed to have been that of the summer house of Zacharias and Elizabeth where the visit of Mary took place — as distinct from the town house where John was born. The Crusader remains include the crypt, the apse and foundations of the walls.

Ein Karem is Hebrew for "Spring of the Vineyard". In the centre of the village is the spring which gives it its name.

BAR'AM

Bar'am, high up in the mountains of Upper Galilee, is the site of the best preserved ancient synagogue in the country, dating to the end of the 2nd or beginning of the 3rd Century A.D. It lies close to the present border with Lebanon, some seven miles northwest of Safad, and is reached, after three miles, by the road that shoots off northwards from Sasa and winds through the picturesque and historic hills.

With the destruction of Jerusalem in 70 A.D., Jewish political and military life was crushed, to flicker briefly only at Massada in the next three years and during the Bar Kochba revolt some 60 years later. But Jewish cultural life was maintained elsewhere in the country, painfully at first, more vigorously later. Its centre was the Galilee.

Only towards the end of the 2nd and beginning of the 3rd Century, however, were the Jewish settlements there allowed to engage in serious rebuilding programmes. This was due largely to the attitude of the Roman emperor Septimius Severus, more benevolent than his predecessors and more tolerant towards the Jews of Palestine. He even gave them encouragement during an extended visit to the country in the year 199. His friendly policy was maintained by his son, Caracalla. It was under their rule that the Jews of Galilee flourished both culturally and economically. Allowed now publicly to develop their communal life, one of their first acts was to construct houses of worship. To this period belong the earliest synagogues in the country, the best preserved being this one at Bar'am and another at Capernaum, on the shores of the Sea of Galilee. They reflect the high level of material culture reached by the Jews at that time. Less well preserved synagogue ruins of the same period are those at Meron, Gush Halav, Khorazin and Arbel. All follow the same structural plan.

The synagogue at Bar'am consisted of an ornate rectangular prayer hall, approached through a covered portico whose roof was supported by pillars. The hall itself was divided by one transverse and two longitudinal rows of columns into a rectangular nave bounded on three sides by aisles. The corner columns stood on heart-shaped bases.

The most impressive part of the structure, which stands to this day, was its main facade. It faces south, towards Jerusalem, site of the destroyed Temple. It has three stone portals. The centre one is the largest and is crowned by a semi-circular arch, decorated with a bas-relief of vine-leaves and clusters of grapes. Part of the ornamented lintel has a sculptured garland set between symbols of victory. A complete stone head of a lion and fragments of a tablet, with symbolic figures for stars, were found among the masonry of the peasants' dwellings in the village of Bar'am. They belonged to the synagogue and had been removed

from the debris when the structure fell into ruin. They were retrieved by the archaeologist, Professor E. L. Sukenik.

A section of the lintel of the facade is now in the Louvre Museum in Paris. It contains this Hebrew inscription: "May there be peace in this place, and in all the places of Israel. This lintel was made by Jose the Levite. Blessings upon his works. Shalom."

HAZOR

Northwards from the Sea of Galilee, the main road winds slowly upwards in a climb from below sea level to the Upper Galilee hills. Nine miles beyond the Sea, just before kibbutz Ayelet Hashahar, it skirts a prominent mound rising above a rectangular plateau. Until recently, there seemed to be nothing special about this locale, covered as it was with scrub and strewn with large boulders. Yet locked within it were the relics of a long history. For this was the site of Biblical Hazor, the city conquered by Joshua, of which it was written "For Hazor beforetime was the head of all those kingdoms." (Joshua, xi, 10).

Hazor was undoubtedly a city of importance in early ages. It is one of the few cities of antiquity in the region cited in pre-Biblical documents from Egypt and Mesopotamia. Its earliest known mention occurs in the 19th Century B.C. Egyptian Execration texts, listing the potential enemies of the Egyptian empire among the distant provinces. Two hundred years later, Hazor is the subject of several letters found in the ancient archives of Mari — the Tell Hariri of today — on the middle Euphrates. Two of these letters inform the king of Mari that messengers from various cities in Mesopotamia are on their way to Hazor. Another letter tells the king that a caravan has arrived from Hazor and Qatna, accompanied by Babylonian envoys. Hazor was indeed the only city in the area mentioned in these documents.

Hazor next finds mention among the cities conquered by the pharaohs Thutmose III, Amenhotep II and Seti I. An interesting allusion to Hazor occurs in the famous 13th Century B.C. Papyrus Anastasi I, in which Hori, a royal official, challenges Amen-em-Opet, a scribe, to answer a number of military and topographical questions. It reads like some ancient military quiz game. One of the questions asked by Hori is: "Where does the *Mahir* (fast military courier) make the journey to Hazor? What is its stream like?".

Perhaps the most important early references to Hazor are those in letters found

11th — 10th Century B.C. bronze figurine of a deity, found at Hazor.

Basalt stele with sculptured hands outstretched in prayer surmounted by emblem
of the deity — a moon disc within a
crescent. Found in 14th–13th Century B.C.
Canaanite Holy of Holies.

in the celebrated 14th Century B.C. archives of el-Amarna, in Egypt. Four of
the letters written to the pharaoh are on the subject of Hazor. One is from the
king of Tyre and one from the king of Astaroth. Both complain that Abdi-
Tarshi, king of Hazor, has rebelled against the pharaoh and captured several
of the complainants' cities. The other two are from the king of Hazor, denying
the charges, reaffirming his loyalty to the Egyptian monarch, and bringing
counter-charges against his accusing neighbours.

But it is in the Biblical narratives that Hazor comes into its own as a key city of
strategic value. The victory of Joshua by the "waters of Merom" marks, according
to the Bible, a decisive phase in the conquest of northern Canaan. Following this
battle, the Bible tells us that "Joshua at that time turned back and took Hazor
and smote the king thereof with the sword: for Hazor beforetime (i.e. no longer
at the time of the narrator but at the time of Joshua) was the head of all those
kingdoms. . . and he burnt Hazor with fire." (Joshua XI, 10–11).
The next mention of Hazor — a passing reference — occurs in the prose account
in chapter four of Judges (as distinct from the Song of Deborah in chapter five)
of the battle which the Israelites fought under the inspiration of Deborah and
the command of Barak. This battle, which took place in "Taanach by the waters
of Megiddo," gave the Israelites their key victory in the final subjugation of the
Canaanites.
Two later Biblical passages make mention of Hazor. Solomon rebuilt "Hazor
and Megiddo and Gezer" (I Kings IX, 15), the three strategic cities dominating
respectively the plains of Huleh, Jezreel and Ayalon (near present day Latrun),
and turned them into royal cities, apparently as garrisons for his hosts of chariots.
This was in the 10th Century B.C. Finally, there is a report of the conquest
of Hazor by the Assyrian king Tiglath Pileser III (II Kings xv, 29). The date of
this conquest was 732 B.C.
Nearly six hundred years later, in 147 B.C., Jonathan the Hasmonean fought
against Demetrius "in the plain of Hazor." This information is recorded in the
First Book of the Maccabees, XI, 63.
In the summer of 1955, a team of Israeli archaeologists, directed by Professor
Yigael Yadin, began a four seasons' dig at this site. This was the James A. de
Rothschild Archaeological Expedition, which carried out the excavations on
behalf of the Hebrew University of Jerusalem and was sponsored by P.I.C.A.,
the Anglo-Israel Exploration Committee and the Government of Israel.
The site is marked by two distinct topographical areas, and both were the subjects
of investigation. One is the Tell — "Tell" is the archaeological term for an
artificial mound covering a buried city or cities. The other is the rectangular
plateau lying to its immediate north.

The Tell is shaped roughly like a bottle, lying from east to west, with its neck at the western end. Its slopes rise steeply from the surrounding wadis to a height of 120 feet. The rectangular plateau is seven times the area of the Tell. Though lower in level, this, too, is high ground, with steep natural slopes on three sides. These slopes were strengthened by artificial embankments, known as glacis. The fourth was the western side, and this was given protection by a formidable wall of beaten earth which rises to a height of 45 feet above the plateau. The thickness at its base is more than 300 feet, and it was further protected by a large moat. Indeed, the earth used to build the wall came from the excavation of the moat. This type of ancient fortification is rare.

Thorough excavations were carried out to the earliest level of settlement in ten specific locations, three on the mound and seven on the rectangular plateau. They uncovered the relics of numerous cities, each layer or stratum containing the remains of a city rebuilt upon the ruins of its predecessor. The more ancient the city, naturally, the lower the level. The city built by Solomon in the 10th Century B.C. was found at the tenth stratum from the surface. Several layers beneath were the charred remains of the last Canaanite city, the one destroyed by fire in Joshua's conquest in the middle of the 13th Century B.C.

The excavations showed that the city of Hazor was first built, on the mound, some time during the first half of the 3rd millennium B.C. — more than four thousand five hundred years ago — in the Early Bronze Age. Only several centuries later, in the 18th Century B.C., was the lower city founded. This was the rectangular plateau. It was at this time that Hazor reached its high point of settlement. With the lower city alone covering an area of 175 acres, it became the largest city in the country and one of the largest in the Middle East; and, as with most large cities of those ages, it was the target of frequent assault. Destroyed and rebuilt, it flourished once more in the 14th Century B.C. — but not for long. Destruction came again at the end of that century. At the beginning of the next, it was re-settled. But though it now covered the same area, its fortifications were less powerful. This was the city that Joshua destroyed, as described in the Bible. Thereafter, the lower city was never again restored. Later rebuilding, notably by king Solomon, was confined to the upper city on the mound alone.

With the collapse of Canaanite rule in Galilee, there were the beginnings of Israelite settlement in Hazor and its surroundings. The archaeological finds revealed that in the century that followed, these settlements were rather poor, reflecting the semi-nomadic character of the new inhabitants. Their living standards and material culture gradually improved, and in the days of Solomon — and after — Hazor developed into a city of some importance. Though now limited to the upper city, and therefore much smaller than it had been between the 18th and

13th centuries, it was no smaller than such other noted Israelite cities as Megiddo, Samaria and Lachish. This importance ended with Tiglath Pileser's conquest. Thereafter, Hazor continued as an open — i.e. unwalled — Jewish settlement that was eventually abandoned. Later, on its site, new citadels were erected by subsequent conquerors of the country during the Persian (587–332 B.C.) and Hellenistic (332–63 B.C.) periods.

Excavations in the southwest corner of the rectangular enclosure yielded startling discoveries during the very first season of digging. The remains of a well-built Canaanite city, with houses and a canalisation system, found only three feet below the surface, were perhaps the most exciting. The floors of the houses were littered with Mycenaean pottery definitely belonging to the 13th Century B.C. This city was destroyed and never again re-settled. Here was the most significant evidence revealed so far supporting the thesis that the date of Joshua's exploits was the 13th Century. (This is an important date, as it helps set the period — still obscure — of several earlier historic events, such as the Exodus of the Children of Israel).

This theory had earlier been severely shaken by the published results of a trial dig carried out on this site in 1928 by the noted British archaeologist, Professor John Garstang. He had apparently not been fortunate in the location he had chosen for his trial excavation, for he came upon no specimens of Mycenaean pottery. In the absence of such pottery, it was reasonable to conclude that the date of the city ruins he uncovered — and therefore of Joshua — must have been earlier than the 13th Century. It was therefore with considerable excitement that Yadin and his team drew forth the vessels and potsherds that lay so near to the surface and found them to be Mycenaean. Later, at other locations, similar pottery was found at this period level. As with oil drillers, one archaeologist may strike treasure only a few hundred yards from the spot where another has encountered only a "dry well".

Excavations at this southwestern location went down to the first city built in the 18th Century, during the Hyksos period, and it was found that the huge earth wall had been constructed at that time. Of the later cities, the most important ruins uncovered here included a small Canaanite "Temple of Stelae" — a stele is an upright slab, often with an inscription or a sculptured relief — unique in Palestinian archaeology and rare in the Middle East. It was built close to the earth wall in the 14th Century and was restored in the 13th. It revealed a branch of Canaanite art on the eve of Joshua's time of which little was known. In the "Holy of Holies" of this temple, apparently dedicated to moon-worship, there was a basalt statuette of a god seated on a throne in the central niche high above the floor. To his left was a row of round-topped stelae of basalt, the middle one bearing a relief of two hands outstretched in prayer, surmounted by an emblem

Winged sphinx and figure kneeling before a "tree of life", carved on 8th Century B.C. ivory box found at Hazor.

of the deity, a moon disc within a crescent. The row of stelae terminated with a basalt orthostat bearing, on its narrow side, the sculptured head and forelegs of a lion, and, on the other, a relief of a crouching lion with tail between its legs. The reliefs are beautifully executed. Also found here was an 18th or 17th Century B.C. jar with a brief cuneiform inscription — the most ancient form of such writing found in the country.

On several of the excavation locations elsewhere on the plateau, at the 17th Century level, burials of infants in large pottery vessels were found beneath the floors of buildings. The remains of a handsome 18th-17th Century palace were discovered in the eastern section. Near it the archaeologists found a series of large burial chambers hewn out of the rock and approached through a network of tunnels. These may have been the family graves of the princes of Hazor.

The crowning discoveries in the lower city were the four temples found at Location H at the northern extremity of the enclosure. The first, built in the 18th-17th Century, consisted of a large hall flanked by two towers and approached across a broad, well-paved square. Stone steps led up to the altar. The second temple, erected in the 15th Century, followed the same architectural design except that the broad square in front of the entrance was now marked by the construction of a monumental gate and several "High Places" and altars. It was in this level that two important relics were found: a baked-pottery model of a cow's liver, used by priests to divine the future, with a long inscription in cuneiform noting the events that were likely to befall; and a bronze tablet with a magnificent relief of what may have been the Canaanite prince or governor. The third temple, belonging to the 14th Century, had a different structural pattern. Instead of the single large hall, it had three chambers, hall, shrine, and the "Holy of Holies", one leading into the other. The lower parts of the walls of both hall and inner sanctum were lined with basalt orthostats. It was in a pit in this temple area and stratum that the scholars found the orthostat of a gate decorated with a fine relief of a lion. It had been buried under stones, no doubt by those who destroyed the temple. The fourth building of worship on this site was a 13th Century restoration of the previous one. Its inner sanctum yielded many objects of worship — a number of them belonging to the earlier temple; an altar bearing the symbol of the sun god; tables for libations and votive offerings; seals and statues. The ruins of this building were found beneath a thick layer of ashes, the result of the burning of the city by Joshua's soldiers.

Excavation of the northeastern corner of the enclosure unearthed the remains of the city gates from all the periods of settlement, making it possible to trace the development of gate-design through five centuries. The earliest, 18th Century, gate was a simple entrance protected by two towers. With the fashioning of more formidable weapons of assault, the later gates had to be strengthened accordingly. The entrance was now through a broad corridor, with two chambers on the right and two on the left; and two large towers, also containing two chambers, protected both sides of the corridor. In front of the gate was a broad terrace and running off it was the approach road for chariots. Supporting both terrace and road was a large retaining wall, built of basalt stones.

The most exciting discovery on the mound, the upper city, found in its western section, were the casemate wall and gate of the city built by Solomon in the 10th Century B.C. The circumstances of the find were also thrilling. As the excavators unearthed the part of the wall that joined what appeared to be the beginning of the gate, Professor Yadin suggested that it might be intriguing to test the following hunch. The Bible recorded that Solomon rebuilt "Hazor and Megiddo and Gezer". The archaeological excavations at Megiddo from 1925–1939 had unearthed the Solomonic gate of that city. Was it not likely, suggested Yadin, that king Solomon's architect may have prepared the same plan in the construction of the city gates of Hazor? They would soon find out. But before digging further, they all thought it would be interesting to mark on the ground the plan of the Megiddo gate, with the corridor, three chambers on either side, and the towers, and see if what they dug up conformed to the markings. They did so; and there, beneath the markings, were the ruins of the very gate construction they had envisaged. It was identical with that at Megiddo. These ruins may be seen today.

Also to be seen are the relics from all period levels excavated here, down to the first settlement more than 4,500 years ago. The most impressive of the earlier remains are those of a large 17th Century B.C. palace, similar to the one found at the same level in the eastern part of the lower city, and a very thick brick wall of the same period; and a large 14th Century palace with orthostats at the entrance, identical with those found in one of the contemporary lower city temples. This was probably the palace of Abdi-Tarshi, the king of Hazor whose letters were found in the el-Amarna archives.

In the post-Solomonic remains, there were some interesting finds which match the reports in the Bible. The city in the stratum belonging to the middle of the 8th Century B.C. — during the reign of Jeroboam II — was found to have been destroyed by earthquake. This earthquake is mentioned in the Book of the prophet Amos (Chapter I, verse 1). The archaeological evidence further disclosed that this Israelite city was quickly rebuilt and that not many years later it was destroyed by fire. This, the work of Tiglath Pileser III in the year 732 B.C., is also recorded in the Bible (II Kings xv, 29). The same Biblical account records that this took place "In the days of Pekah king of Israel"; and, indeed, one of the wine jars found here bore the Hebrew inscription: "Pekah's".

Basalt statue of Canaanite god, found in sanctuary of 14th-13th Century B.C.

Excavations at this location offered further evidence of the new techniques in fortification which were evolved in the periods after Solomon. In his time, the casemate wall with its hollow chambers was considered sufficient protection against contemporary assault weapons. In the following century, however, as was first pointed out by Yadin, the development of a more powerful battering ram rendered the casemate type of fortification inadequate, and it was replaced by a huge solid wall with characteristic salients and recesses. In some cases, as a transitional device, the hollow chambers in the casemate were filled in. Examples of both were found in this western section of the Hazor mound and may be seen on the site. There are parts of the Solomonic casemate wall which had been filled in during the 9th Century; and there are remains of the solid wall, to which it had given way in the 8th Century, built by the Israelites on the eve of the Assyrian attack.

On this site, too, remains were unearthed of a series of citadels, each erected on the ruins of its predecessor, dating from the 9th to the 2nd Century B.C. The earliest, built and strengthened by the Israelite kings who followed Solomon, was a square fort, with rows of square rooms on the north and south sides and two long narrow halls between them. Much of the area of the citadel was taken up by solid walls. The strong foundations extended ten feet below the floor. The later citadels belong to the Assyrian, Persian and Hellenistic periods.

Incidentally, the nearby building with pillars — these look like hitching posts, which led Garstang erroneously to attribute them to stables — was found to have been a large Israelite storehouse. It was built in the 9th Century, probably during the reign of Ahab (869–850 B.C.).

At the eastern edge of the mound, the archaeologists found a small gate built of large ashlar stones. Shortly before the 732 B.C. destruction of the city, the Israelites in Hazor had hurriedly blocked this gate with bricks, and had camouflaged it on the outside — the side facing a potential enemy — with a thin layer of rubble. This small gate was probably opened in the wall during a quiet period in the 8th Century to make it easier for the farmers of Hazor to bring in the wheat from their extensive fields to the immediate north. On the eve of the siege, it could no longer serve this purpose. It now became a point of weakness in their defences and an obvious target of enemy assault. It was therefore hastily sealed. Supporting the theory that this was the farmers' gate was the discovery close by of a large rectangular grain silo, 16 feet deep, its sides lined with rough stones. The floor was covered by a thick layer of fine ash, remains of the grain burnt when the city was destroyed.

This, then, was Hazor of old, Hazor which "beforetime was the head of all those kingdoms."

Stone incense ladle, in form of hand clasping bowl, found in 8th Century B.C. Israelite citadel.

SAFAD

Mountainous Upper Galilee, fragrant and alive with colour at all seasons, is studded with villages and hamlets which cling to the rocky slopes. None is more picturesque than its capital, Safad. It is the northernmost town in Israel, and the highest, sitting atop an elevation more than 2,700 feet above sea level. There is an ineffable enchantment about Safad that becomes almost tangible the moment you enter one of its cobbled alleyways, descend the steps to the artists' quarter, or come upon one of its ancient synagogues. This strange quality, which has given the city a power of attraction to both pious scholar and bohemian painter, is compounded of many elements. It has at once the splendour and quaintness of any city perched upon a mountain top. Narrow lanes and crooked stairways branch off the main road which winds through the town and encircles the citadel on the summit. The buildings blend into the hillside, some of them touched by architectural artistry. The light seems charged with a special luminosity. The air is clear and fresh. In summer it is a cool haven from the hot plain below. There is a breath of magic about this Galilean city.

It stands on the ancient highway from Damascus in Syria to Acre on Israel's Mediterranean coast, and is located some ten miles northwest of the Sea of Galilee and the same distance southwest of the Huleh. It is best reached from Tiberias, nearly 700 feet below sea level. The ascent is spectacular, the road climbing more than 3,000 feet over a distance of twenty-one miles.

The finest view from Safad is the southern panorama. This can best be seen from the citadel summit. In the immediate foreground are the flat tops of the houses, with their interior courtyards, which hug the terraced slopes. Beyond is the valley, made green by Israel's pioneer settlements, which extends from the northern part of Kinneret, where the Jordan falls into the Lake, southwards to the redoubtable Horns of Hattin.

In the heart of the old city stand the synagogues of Safad, windows to life in the Middle Ages. Rembrandt-like figures may still be seen against the Ark of the Law, poring in reverent study over the holy tomes. This is the Safad which drew to itself in the 16th Century A.D. a band of pious scholars and Cabbalists, who studied and argued, read and wrote holy books, and sought to unlock the secret of life.

That century, following the Jewish expulsion from Spain, was the golden age of the city of Safad. It was during this period that the northern Galilean town became the seat, centre and geographic fountain-head of the Cabbalists, the small but potent group of pious scholars who devoted themselves to the regeneration of Jewish oral tradition, who delved into esoteric doctrine, and who sought to fathom occult lore and interpret Jewish mysticism. The purity and vigorous

freshness of its mountain air were among Safad's attractions. There has always been a profound belief that "the air of the Holy Land maketh man wise", and in Safad "there is the purest air in the Holy Land". This, the Cabbalists held, would enable them more readily and clearly to understand the hidden meanings of the Holy Book.

Its proximity to the tomb of Rabbi Shimon Bar Yochai, buried in nearby Meron, is probably the prime reason why Safad became the gathering place for these Jewish scholars. He is believed to have been the author of the basic book of the Cabbalists, the Zohar, or The Book of Splendour. This is a mystical commentary on the Five Books of Moses which proceeds from the premise that every letter, word and line in the Law of God is significant, and contains a deeper meaning. To the initiated, this offers the key to the secret of life. With the Jewish expulsion from Spain, the Zohar soon achieved an importance as a work of study second only to the Talmud. For the expulsion was considered as the darkest hour before the dawn, obviously to be followed by the coming of the Redeemer, as the Prophets of old had foretold. And so, as the distinguished Jewish historian Dr. Cecil Roth points out, scholars of a mystic turn of mind "directed their steps with one accord to Upper Galilee, where the action of the Book of Splendour was staged, where its saintly author had lived, and where his grave was still revered." Traditional Jewish life was lived in Safad with intensity, with mystical fervour, and with a meticulous and scrupulous adherence to precept.

The key Cabbala figure who personified these tendencies and who made the decisive impact on Safad in the sixteenth century was Rabbi Isaac Luria. Born in Jerusalem but educated in Egypt, he became engrossed in the study of the Zohar. Leaving his fellow men, he lived the life of a hermit for several years, spending his days and nights in meditation over the secret and special wisdom of this great book. He then left the banks of the Nile for the "Holy City" of Safad and there gathered about him a group of faithful Cabbalistic disciples. To them he was known as Our Master, which in Hebrew is Adonenu. The A of Adonenu plus the initials of Rabbi Isaac form the word ARI — which is Hebrew for Lion. He was thus known as Ha'Ari. And his disciples were called The Young Lions — Gurei Ha'Ari in Hebrew.

Among the many other Rabbis and scholars whose lives and work enriched the city of Safad, the most noted is Rabbi Yosef Caro, author of the Shulchan Aruch. This is the great work of methodic codification of Jewish religious practice, embracing every phase in the life of the pious Jew, in the home and in the office, in the synagogue and in the court of law. It is, to this day, the standard text and guide in Jewish religious communities all over the world. It is the product of immense scholarship, erudition and research. Yosef Caro wrote this magnum opus in Safad, completing it in 1563.

On the summit of Mount Safad are the scattered ruins of a Crusader castle, built in the 12th Century to command the highway from Damascus, where the Moslems were entrenched. In an earlier age, the 1st Century A.D., the Jews of Galilee built their citadel here. They did so under the direction of Josephus — before he changed his ways and before he wrote his great works — when he was sent north to prepare them for the revolt against the Romans. Today the site is covered by a memorial park to those who fell in the 1948 capture of Safad during Israel's War of Independence.

Of the synagogues, the three oldest are the two synagogues of Ha'Ari, one Sephardi and one Ashkenazi, where the Lion used to pray, and the Bennia synagogue named after Rabbi Yossie Bennia who is buried nearby. All three are small, simple and intimate, producing a mediaeval atmosphere of austere piety and of a direct communion between man and God. The Arks contain comparatively old Scrolls of the Law and the walls are lined with Biblical and Talmudic books and commentaries. It is not difficult, entering these synagogues from the bright sunlight outside, to conjure up the sixteenth century vision of saintly scholars, surrounded by their disciples, gathering here for prayer, and later, seated near the Holy Ark, engaging in mystical discourses on the secrets of God's meaning.

On the slope below these synagogues, facing Meron, is the Jewish cemetery, where lie buried the Lion himself, Rabbi Yosef Caro, and the other Talmudic luminaries of the sixteenth century who made Safad great.

MERON

On a mountain slope facing Safad, and five and a half miles away to the northwest by road, lies Meron, kindred centre, with Safad, of the Cabbalists, burial place of renowned ancient Rabbis, and the site of some fine and well-preserved mediaeval buildings.

Its interest for the Cabbalists is natural. Its central shrine houses the remains of Rabbi Shimon bar Yochai, the 2nd Century Talmudic scholar and mystic who is credited with authorship of the Zohar, the Book of Splendour. A fervent fighter for Jewish independence, he was at one time forced to flee the wrath of the Romans, hiding in a Galilean cave with his son Eleazar. It was here, according to tradition, that he wrote that classic work.

The tomb in the centre of the shrine is that of Rabbi Shimon. The second, in

Carved stone facade of 2nd–3rd Century synagogue at Meron.

the corner, is that of his son Eleazar. The mediaeval building housing the tombs is topped by a large cupola, flanked by two pillars on which rest stone basins. Access to these pillars on the roof is gained directly from the courtyard by the original stone steps.

A little way to the north are the remains of a 2nd Century synagogue with a stone facade, its doorways facing south, towards Jerusalem. It was a simple rectangular structure with a nave bounded by eighteen columns.

Nearby is the tomb of an interesting 2nd Century Rabbi who combined scholarship with craftsmanship. Though an outstanding Talmudic figure, whose writings are familiar to Rabbinical students to this day, only his first name is known — Yohanan — Hebrew for John. He practised the Talmudic injunction that all should learn to master a trade. The trade he chose was shoe-making, and he divided his time between The Book and the last. He was thus always referred to as Rabbi Yohanan Ha'Sandlar — Rabbi John the cobbler. (Sandlar is Hebrew for cobbler). The cave near the tomb is said to have been his workshop.

The two remaining sites of interest in Meron are believed to be the burial places of the two outstanding 1st Century B. C. sages, Hillel and Shammai. Both were Talmudic giants, whose writings and sayings reflect extraordinary erudition and deep wisdom. Both were founders of new schools of thought which had their impact on scholars for centuries. Shammai was noted for his toughness in Biblical interpretation, Hillel for his gentleness. "Do not unto others what you would not have others do unto you" is Hillel's. This basic principle of human behaviour was his response to the man who asked to be taught the fundamentals of Judaism "while standing on one leg". Hillel and his disciples are believed to have been buried in a cave not far from the site where, two centuries later, Rabbi Yohanan was laid to rest. At all events, mediaeval pilgrims referred to it as "Hillel's Cave". Shammai's burial place is believed to be the rectangular two-storeyed tomb on the hill facing the shrine of Rabbi Shimon bar Yochai.

Once a year, Meron is the scene of a vast religious pilgrimage when thousands of orthodox families come to pay homage at the tomb of Rabbi Shimon. The day is called in Hebrew Lag Ba'Omer, celebrated 33 days after the commencement of the Festival of Pesach (Passover). It is a joyous holiday, whose origins are obscure. Rabbi Shimon is believed to have died on this day, and entered the Divine Presence. It was therefore chosen by the Cabbalists of Safad in the 16th Century as a day not of mourning but of gay celebration, marked by religious song and dance round the tomb of the holy Rabbi. The custom is maintained to this day. Shortly before sundown, the orthodox men, women and children gather in the sepulchre and pray. After dark, bonfires are lit in the stone basins on the roof and kept going all through the night, while the pilgrims dance to mediaeval Jewish melodies and sing hymns of praise.

SEA OF GALILEE

The Sea of Galilee, a harp-shaped lake of blue set in Israel's sun-drenched Jordan Valley, is swept by history. This was the stage whereon were enacted great events in ages past which stirred the minds of men down the centuries. The timeless tales are recorded in the Scriptures. Their setting is still a scene of wonder. The ancient Rabbis used to say that "Jehovah hath created seven seas, but the Sea of Galilee is His delight." The historian Josephus marvelled at its equable climate in winter. "The temper of the air is so well blended," he wrote. "One may call this place the ambition of Nature. . . it is a happy contention of the seasons. . ."

An early traveller gave this description: "Whether approached at sunrise, when the sun appears suddenly from behind the hills on the eastern shore, lighting small fishing craft casting far out into the deep, or at solemn sunset when the blue-green waters are ruffled with colour and life as they play about the tumbled, stone quays of long abandoned towns, its shores and waters preserve the atmosphere of peace and storm, success and doom."

At the close of the last century, the eloquent and seemingly omniscient George Adam Smith, a meticulous observer with a spare recording style, was inspired to write: "Sweet water, full of fish, a surface of sparkling blue, tempting down breezes from above, bringing forth breezes of her own, the Lake of Galilee is at once food, drink and air, a rest to the eye, coolness in the heat. . . and a facility of travel very welcome. . ."

Two thousand years ago the Sea of Galilee was fringed with fertile plantations of palms, vineyards, olive groves, walnut and fig trees. The lakeside hummed with the movement of fishermen and boat-builders. There were nine cities, the most important, then as now, being Tiberias, on the western shore. Then came the decline, and for centuries the area lapsed into the desolation of swamp and marsh. Only in this century has the ancient fruitfulness been revived by the new pioneers of Israel. It was here that they founded the first cooperative farm village, kibbutz Degania, in 1909. Today, as in ancient times, the land around the Sea of Galilee gives forth its abundance, the water its yields of fish, and the lakeside echoes to the happy laughter of holidaymakers at play.

The Sea of Galilee has many names. In the Old Testament books of Numbers and Deuteronomy, it is known as the Sea of Chinnereth. In Joshua it is called Chinneroth. The origin is Chinor, Hebrew for harp, and it is believed to have been so named because of its shape. A later legend ascribed the origin to its association with the gentle lapping of the water which was "as sweet as the voice of the harp." In the New Testament it is referred to variously as the Sea of Galilee, the Sea of Tiberias, Lake Tiberias, the Lake or Sea of Gennesaret, or quite simply

as "the lake" or "the sea". Today it is called the Sea of Galilee, Lake Kinneret or Lake Tiberias.

The Sea of Galilee, in northeastern Israel, lies 689 feet below sea level, which makes it the most popular winter resort area in the country, with warm temperatures from autumn to spring. It is a little over 32 miles in circumference, 13 miles long and, at its broadest, 8 miles. In general it is a calm lake; but on occasion it is subject to violent storms, just as it was, from the Biblical accounts, in days gone by. It is fed partly by natural springs but mostly by the waters of the Jordan.

The most noted sites of antiquity around the Sea of Galilee are Tiberias, Beth Yerach, Capernaum, Tabgha and the Mount of the Beatitudes. There are, however, also several less well-known sites which have been the subject of fruitful archaeological excavation or which are associated with historic events. Of these, the most interesting are Khorazin, Minya, Wadi Amud, Magdala, Arbel, Sha'ar Hagolan, Ein Gev and Sussita.

The basalt ruins of Khorazin and its celebrated 3rd Century A.D. synagogue are located two and a half miles to the north of the northern shore of the Lake, about half a mile east of the Tiberias-Rosh Pinna highway. Little is known of this ancient city — also called Korazim and Chorazin — beyond the facts that it was a small Jewish town noted for the excellence of its wheat, and that it was frequented by Jesus. From the New Testament we know that he prayed and preached in the local synagogue — an earlier one, of course, than that which we now see in ruins. But apparently to little effect. His "Woe unto thee, Chorazin. . ." is recorded in Matthew (XI, 21).

Archaeological excavations revealed an abundance of prehistoric relics, showing that Khorazin was a site of settlement from earliest times. The ruins visible today, however, are those of a later city which continued in existence up to the 4th Century A.D. Excavations are continuing under the direction of archaeologist Ze'ev Yeivin. The most interesting ruins are those of the synagogue. Still standing are parts of the walls of the rectangular prayer hall, the floor, and the pedestals of ten of the original fourteen columns. Nearby are parts of broken pillars and capitals. Some of the basalt stones are decorated with reliefs. One of them has been sculptured into a primitive representation of the Lion of Judah.

One of the most interesting finds was a beautifully fashioned stone chair, with a dedicatory inscription in Judaeo-Aramaic. This is believed by some scholars to have been intended as the "Cathedra (Chair) of Moses", mentioned in Talmudic literature, and installed in ancient synagogues as the seat of honour for the head of the community. The chair has been removed to Jerusalem where it is on permanent exhibition in the Antiquities Museum.

Four miles southwest of Khorazin, near the edge of the lake, are the ruins of Minya. The best preserved remains are those of a large palace built by one of the Umayyad caliphs in the 7th Century A.D., no doubt as a winter retreat. What is left of it shows that it was a splendid structure, square in shape, with round towers at each corner, spacious dwelling rooms with mosaic floors of geometric design, and a private mosque — the oldest in Israel. Not far off to the north are the ruins of a much later building, a Turkish caravanserai, known as Khan Minya, which served travellers using the main road through Palestine to Damascus. It was clearly a wayside station of some importance, sufficient at all events so to impress a 17th Century traveller that he referred to the Sea of Galilee as the Sea of Minya.

On the other side of the main road, due west of Khan Minya, is Wadi Amud, a gorge noted for its prehistoric caves. It was in one of these that the 100,000 years old Palaeolithic skull was found in 1925, the oldest human skull discovered up to then in the country. It is known popularly as "Galilee Man". (In 1959, however, part of a very much older skull was discovered at Ubeidiye, in the Jordan Valley, just south of the Sea of Galilee. It is believed to be half a million years old, and it may well be the most important prehistoric find in the country. The discovery was made by Professor M. Stekelis, the Hebrew University's archaeologist of the prehistoric period.) In 1961, the caves of Wadi Amud were the scene of renewed archaelogical study. Following a survey and trial dig by a Japanese scholar, Hitoshi Watanabi, which showed undisturbed palaeolithic deposits, Professor Hitashi Suzuki headed a Tokyo University Expedition which started a season of excavation on the site. Their most important find was a fairly complete skeleton of an adult male whose cranium bore all the characteristics of Neanderthal Man.

One mile south of Wadi Amud, also on the landward side of the Tiberias-Rosh Pinna road, is Migdal, traditional site of Magdala and birthplace of Mary Magdalena (i.e. Mary of Magdala). "Mary called Magdalena, out of whom went seven devils", was one of the women "which had been healed of evil spirits and infirmities", and "which followed Jesus from Galilee, ministering unto him". (Luke VIII, 2, and Matthew XXVII, 55.) In the latter part of the Second Temple period, this village was known as Migdal Nunaya in Hebrew and Taricheae in Greek — the place for the salting of fish. As Taricheae it figures prominently in Josephus' "The Wars of the Jews" and would appear from his narrative to have been a considerable town in the 1st Century A.D. It was one of the sites which he fortified when he was governor of Galilee — before his defection to the Romans. It is the setting of an exciting episode — recounted in Book 2, Chapter 21 — in which Josephus claims to have discomfited a "mob whipped up by John", John of Gischala, the fervent Jewish patriot who considered

Josephus a traitor, fought him bitterly and sought to get him deposed. Josephus describes how "the crowd packed the Hippodrome at Taricheae and filled the air with yells of rage, some clamouring to stone the 'traitor', others to burn him alive". Into this howling mob steps Josephus, showing, as he says of himself, "no trace of fear". He saves the day — and his life — by conceiving "a stratagem by which he would induce his enraged critics to quarrel among themselves". He was neither the first nor the last leader to follow the principle Divide and Rule. Some years later, during the 66–70 A.D. struggle of the Jews against the Romans, Taricheae fell to Titus in a key battle, the Jewish dead totalling 6,700. "After the battle, Vespasian (father of Titus) held a court-martial in Taricheae . . . The aged and useless, 1,200 of them, were disposed of by his orders. From the young men he picked out the 6,000 strongest and sent them to Nero at the Isthmus (as navvies to dig the Corinth Canâl). The rest of the people, to the number of 30,400, he auctioned . . ." (Book 3, Chapter 10.)

Two miles southwest of Migdal and poised dramatically on the edge of a sheer cliff is the ancient site of Arbel. As the centre of a flourishing agricultural area — Arbel was noted for its linen, woven from the flax grown in the valley below — and strategically situated to command a subsidiary route from Galilee to the Mediterranean coast, it was a city of some importance as far back as the latter part of the Second Temple period. The Jews of Arbel put up a tough resistance against the Syrian invader during the victorious struggle of Judah the Maccabee in the middle of the 2nd Century B.C. A hundred years later, their descendants fought valiantly, but hopelessly, against Herod when he was battling, with Roman support, to usurp the throne from Mattathias Antigonus. The suicidal stand of the Jews of Arbel, who held out in the cliffside caves below the city and stubbornly spurned Herod's appeal to them to surrender, is movingly recorded by Josephus. (Wars of the Jews, Book I, Chapter 16.) Arbel maintained its fighting tradition in the final Jewish revolt against the Romans in 66 A.D. Remains of subsequent Jewish settlement may be seen today. They include ruins of a city wall, buildings, wells, a large cistern hewn out of the rock, and a 3rd Century A.D. synagogue.

Two miles southwest of Arbel loom the Horns of Hattin, the curiously shaped ridge, like the profile of animal horns, of a once volcanic hill. It was at the foot of this hill that the Crusaders suffered their decisive defeat at the hands of Saladin in 1187 A.D.

Kibbutz Sha'ar Hagolan, between the Yarmuk river and the southern shore of the Lake, maintains a museum with a unique collection of finds discovered in the area. Excavations carried out in 1949–52 by the archaeologist of the prehistoric period, Professor M. Stekelis, of the Hebrew University, brought to light evidence of a Neolithic culture, dating to about 5000 B.C., unparalleled by any

9000-year old female figurine, etched on a pebble, used in Neolithic fertility rites. Found at Sha'ar Hagolan.

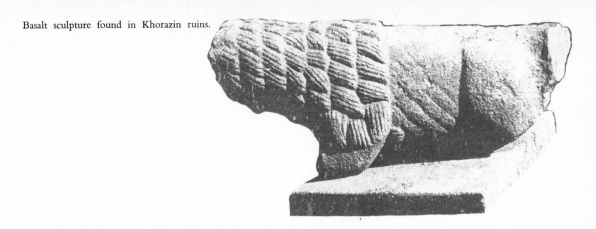

other Neolithic settlement in the country. (It is now known as the "Yarmuk Culture"). He found numerous farming implements as well as ritual objects pointing to the celebration of agricultural fertility rites, clear evidence of a settled community who worked the land.

Across the water from Tiberias, midway along the eastern shore of the Sea of Galilee, is kibbutz Ein Gev, a charming farm settlement noted for its fishing, its bananas, its dates, and its annual music festival in a sumptuous lakeside auditorium. Founded in 1937, it was the first Zionist settlement to be established on the eastern edge of the lake.

An artificial mound within its estate, clearly containing remains of ancient habitation, had long interested archaeologists. Not until 1961, however, were excavations carried out on this Tell. The team of scholars was headed by Professor Benjamin Mazar, of the Hebrew University.

They unearthed five layers of settlement, each short-lived, the oldest dating back to the 10th Century B.C. This was a walled city, built during the reign of David or Solomon, at a time when Israelite rule extended east of the Jordan and as far north as Damascus. The next city, built on its ruins at the end of the 10th or the beginning of the 9th Century B.C., was fortified by a casemate wall. It was at this time, the archaeologists believe, that the defences were strengthened by the construction of the citadel on the high ground to the north of the compound. It proved of little avail. For this city was destroyed, apparently by Ben Haddad I, king of Syria, in 886 B.C.

After a brief period of abandonment, it was rebuilt in the middle of the 9th Century, in the days of the Israelite king Omri or Ahab. The earlier casemate wall had now given way to a solid wall with salients and recesses. Among the many artefacts found in this stratum was a pottery vessel with an inscription in early Hebrew. This city, too, lasted only a short time, having been destroyed, probably by the army of Shelmanassar III, in 838 B.C. It too was soon rebuilt, again destroyed and again rebuilt. Final destruction came in 732 B.C., with the invasion of the Assyrian emperor Tiglath Pileser III.

Rising above Ein Gev, among the lower slopes of the towering Golan mountains, is a hill 600 feet high known as Sussita. This is the site of an ancient city with a longer history than that of the settlement in the Tell below. Sussita was held by the Talmudic sages to have been the centre of the area associated with the early life of Jephtha the Judge. Its name is derived from "suss", Hebrew for "horse", because of the equine line of its summit. The same idea prompted its Greek name — Hippos — during the Hellenistic period, and as Hippos it appears as one of the "league of ten cities", the Decapolis. In the 66 A.D. Jewish revolt against the Romans, its Hellenised community found favour in the eyes of their Roman masters by taking up arms against their Jewish neighbours. Some years after the

Roman destruction of Jerusalem, Jews resettled in and around Sussita, among them several sages. Most of the Jews there lived by farming.

Remains of this early period may be seen on the hill today. With natural defence offered by steep slopes on three sides, the strongest part of the city's encircling wall was in the east, to protect the comparatively easy access from that direction across a short spur which links the hill to the mountain range. The site contains ruins of this wall and of several buildings, a water cistern, pillars, capitals and a variety of sculptured stones. Habitation continued up to the Moslem conquest in the 7th Century A.D., and relics have been found of a theatre, paved streets and three Byzantine churches dating to the 5th and 6th Centuries A.D.

CAPERNAUM

There is frequent mention of the Sea of Galilee in the New Testament as the scene both of miracles and of prosaic events in the lives of the founder of Christianity and His disciples. It was while Jesus was "walking by the Sea of Galilee" that he "saw two brethren, Simon called Peter, and Andrew his brother, casting a net into the sea: for they were fishers. And he saith unto them, Follow me, and I will make you fishers of men." (Matthew, ɪv, 18, 19).

On the northern edge of the lake is the site where Jesus came when He left Nazareth to begin His mission. This is Capernaum, of which it is written: "And they went into Capernaum; and straightway on the sabbath day he entered into the synagogue, and taught". (Mark ɪ, 21). To this day, at Capernaum, on the very edge of the Sea, stand the ruins of an ancient synagogue. Though it was built in the 2nd-3rd Century, there is reason to believe that it was erected close to the House of Prayer where Jesus preached.

Capernaum is the Greek spelling for the Hebrew name of the site — Kfar Nahum, the village of Nahum. It was a reasonably well known townlet in the time of Jesus, standing close to the highway which ran northeastwards from the lake into lower Syria. It was here that Jesus made His home in His early years. It was here that He healed the servant of the centurion. Capernaum lapsed into decline in the 6th Century. The Franciscan Order purchased the site from the Turks in 1894 and erected a monastery close to the synagogue ruins.

These are in a good state of preservation and contain richly carved lintels and friezes, decorated arches, sculptured capitals, and stone benches for the wor-

Sculptured palm tree on capital in 2nd–3rd Century synagogue of Capernaum.

The "Ark of the Covenant", sculptured in form of a temple set on wheels, at Capernaum.

shippers. The large rectangular prayer hall was divided by columns, as at Bar'am, into nave and three aisles. The Ark containing the Scrolls of the Law stood in front of the south wall of the nave, facing Jerusalem. The floor was paved with large slabs of stone. The roof and second storey of this structure are missing. Running off the eastern wall was a large annexe in the form of a trapezium, with covered aisles round an open court. This two-storeyed white synagogue on the lakeside, contrasting with the black basalt of the region, must have been an impressive sight, well matching its imposing interior.

The prevailing design of the stone carvings, excellent examples of the art of the period, are palm trees, clusters of grapes, eagles with spread wings, and the traditional seven-branched candelabrum, the menora, which is today the emblem of the State of Israel. Characteristic is the lintel decoration above the main entrance — an eagle flanked by palm trees. (The palm was the symbol of the Land of Israel and appears on many ancient Jewish coins). Occasionally there are other themes, like the sculptured sea-shell set in a garland of flowers which adorns the keystone of the arch above the central door. The best preserved relief of a candelabrum is to be seen on one of the stone capitals, together with a shofar, the ram's horn of Jewish ritual, on which was to be sounded the call for Israel's redemption.

Of special interest is the sculpture of a frieze-stone which rested on the capital of a pilaster. It is in the form of an ancient temple on chariot wheels. Interpretations differ, but it probably represented the Ark of the Covenant, the artist adding wheels to give it the appearance of a distinguished contemporary vehicle.

Apart from the numerous sections of columns, Corinthian capitals, Attic bases, and portions of decorative masonry strewn about the synagogue compound, relics were found on the site of basalt implements used by the ancient inhabitants, including a large oil press and grain mills.

TABGHA

Close to Capernaum, and to its west, also on the edge of the north shore, is Tabgha, traditional site of the miracle of the loaves and fishes. The story is told in Matthew (xv), Mark (viii), Luke (ix) and John (vi) — most succinctly in verses 11–17 of Luke.

The apostles had been sent on missionary journeys. When they returned, they

4th Century mosaic at Tabgha depicting the "miracle of the loaves and fishes".

met with Jesus to make their reports at what was to have been a private gathering. But the local populace soon began to descend on the meeting place, and Jesus "received them, and spake unto them. . . and healed them that had need of healing." As the day wore on, the apostles suggested that the crowd be sent away, "that they may go into the towns and country round about, and lodge, and get victuals," for there was no food for them. But Jesus said: "Give ye them to eat. And they said, We have no more but five loaves and two fishes . . . For they were about five thousand men. And he said to his disciples, Make them sit down by fifties in a company. And they did so, and made them all sit down. Then he took the five loaves and the two fishes, and looking up to heaven, he blessed them, and brake, and gave to the disciples to set before the multitude. And they did eat, and were all filled: and there was taken up of fragments that remained to them twelve baskets."

The story of this miracle is commemorated in a beautifully preserved 5th Century mosaic at Tabgha, the principal ornamental feature of the Byzantine Church of the Multiplication which was erected on this site. The Byzantine structure has long since crumbled to dust, but a new church has been built over the mosaics and a remnant of the original altar.

The mosaic of the Multiplication is a well executed but primitive representation of a basket of loaves set between two fish. Far more sophisticated is the decorative floor mosaic at the left of the altar, laid down in the following century. For motif the artist chose birds and plants which are indigenous to the nearby Huleh. (In the recent clearance of the Huleh marsh, a small area was left as a bird sanctuary). Prominent among the mosaic's flora are lotus and oleander. Moving among them are the heron, dove and cormorant, fat geese and squat ducklings. Two peacocks face each other at the foot of the main panel.

MOUNT OF THE BEATITUDES

Rising above Tabgha is a gentle hill covered with grass, though still strewn, as in ages past, with huge boulders. The summit of this hill is the traditional spot where Jesus, looking out over the waters of the Lake, uttered the immortal words of His Sermon on the Mount: "Blessed are the poor in spirit: for theirs is the kingdom of heaven. . . Blessed are the meek: for they shall inherit the earth. . ." This is the Mount of the Beatitudes.

"It is a sweet spot", as an early traveller recorded, and the view southwards is impressive, taking in the blue expanse of the Sea of Galilee and the purple heights of the eastern Gaulan mountains. In the still of eventide, as the sun sheds its last glory, every syllable voiced from the summit can be heard distinctly at the foot of the Mount. Thus it must have been when Jesus spoke.

Only the site is ancient — the mound and the stones. There is no relic of any early structure commemorating the event. But today the Mount is crowned by a circular Church of the Beatitudes, built by the Franciscans in 1937. It contains symbolic representations of the Seven Virtues — charity, justice, prudence, hope, faith, fortitude and temperance.

TIBERIAS

Tiberias, the capital of Galilee, is situated midway along the western shore of the Lake. It was built by Herod Antipas, Tetrarch of Galilee and son of king Herod the Great, in the 1st Century A.D. and named in honour of the Roman emperor Tiberius. Later, however, inventive Rabbis suggested an ingenious Hebrew origin of "Tiberias" (whose spelling is also different from that of the emperor's name). It derived, they said, from Tabur, Hebrew for navel. This reflected the central place occupied by Tiberias in Jewish life after the destruction of the Jerusalem Temple.

Certain it is that after the Jews of Jerusalem had been crushed by the Romans, Galilee superseded Judah as the principal area of Jewish settlement. Tiberias became the seat of Jewish learning and the dwelling place of the great sages. It was here that the Palestinian (better but less accurately known as the "Jerusalem") Talmud, as distinct from the Babylonian Talmud, was compiled. (The Talmud is the fabulous commentary on the Mishnah, comprehensive and discursive, which encompasses the whole of the early wisdom of the Jewish people. The Mishnah is the codification of the traditional Jewish jurisprudence, and was completed at the end of the 2nd Century at Sepphoris, about fifteen miles west of Tiberias.) It was in Tiberias, too, that the vowel and punctuation system of the Hebrew script was devised in the 8th Century. In the 16th Century, there was an influx of scholars and Rabbis from Spain, following the expulsion of the Jews from that country, and they enriched the spiritual life of Tiberias.

Small wonder that some of the most venerated sites of antiquity in the city are the

Domed shrine of Rabbi Meir Baal Haness, 2nd Century A.D. scholar, "giver of light" and "maker of miracles".

tombs of Jewish scholars. On the slope of a hill overlooking Tiberias lies the great Rabbi Akiva, noted for his immense learning and his political courage. He it was who placed his vast spiritual weight behind the revolt of Bar Kochba against the Romans in the year 132 A.D. in the struggle for Jewish freedom. They held out for three years, succeeding even in recapturing Jerusalem for a short while. The rebellion was crushed in the year 135, and Akiva, captured by the conquerors, was cruelly put to death.

Tiberias contains the shrine of Rabbi Yohanan Ben Zakkai, the most eminent scholar of the 1st Century, and founder of the great academy of Yavne. Buried nearby are the 3rd Century sages, Rabbis Ami and Assi. So pious were they, but so absorbed in study, that it was said of them that "though they had thirteen synagogues in Tiberias in which to recite their prayers, they prayed only between the pillars of their study-room." One of the holiest sanctuaries is the tomb with the twin cupolas on the rising ground above the shore line. Here lie the remains of Rabbi Meir Baal Haness. Baal Haness is the Hebrew for "maker of miracles"; Meir means "giver of light". This 2nd century scholar was believed to be so profound that he "gave light" even to sages.

The memorial site which attracts most visitors is the tomb of the incredible 12th Century scholar, Rabbi Moses Ben Maimon, more familiarly known by the Greek form, Maimonides, or by the acronym derived from the Hebrew capitals of his name, the Rambam. Ben Maimon was the commanding intellectual of his age, physician and philosopher, writer and savant, whose encyclopaedic and logical mind absorbed and simplified the complexities of both medicine and Jewish scholarship. His medical treatises were widely translated. He was court doctor to Saladin in Cairo. (It is said that during the Third Crusade, Saladin's foe, Richard the Lion Heart, sought unsuccessfully to persuade him to return to England with him). In the field of Jewish learning, he wrote his celebrated Mishneh Torah, in which he reduced to simple and methodical terms the whole of the traditional Jewish teaching as expressed in the Talmud. His greatest and best known work is *Guide of the Perplexed,* a presentation of the philosophy of Judaism.

Though Tiberias, the city which achieved some prominence in history, was built by Herod Antipas, the site had been settled many centuries earlier. The main attraction was its hot sulphur springs, noted in olden times for their powers of healing, and very much in use today by the tens of thousands who come annually to take the cure. Herod Antipas built his palace nearby no doubt to take advantage of the beneficial waters. The city that arose on this spot in Biblical times, as we know from the Book of Joshua (XIX, 35), was appropriately called Hammath. For "ham" in Hebrew means "hot". Today, the baths are known as "Hamei Tiberias".

What are believed to be the ruins of ancient Hammath were discovered during recent archaeological excavations carried out by Dr. Moshe Dothan, on behalf of the Antiquities Department, in the mound adjoining the thermal springs compound. The antiquities include the southern gate of the city and the baths of the Israelite period. The most notable discovery, however, was the 4th Century A.D. synagogue with a mosaic floor which, from the technical point of view, is about the best early synagogue mosaic in the country. The top panel shows the Ark of the Law, set between two familiar seven-branched candelabra. Less familiar, however, is the artistry whereby the mouth of each branch seems to give off a flickering light. The motif of the large central panel is the signs of the Zodiac, decorated with sophisticated figures of humans and animals. One of the them, a lion, has a richly coloured mane, and whiskers that positively bristle. The subtleties of light and shade come through admirably in this mosaic. At an upper level are the remains of a later synagogue, with mosaics of conventional geometric design.

The curative baths together with the tropical climate of this sub-sea-level lake make Tiberias a popular health spa throughout the year and an attractive holiday resort in the winter. It is served by modern hotels, gracious parks, open air quay-side restaurants, and facilities for swimming, fishing, boating, water-skiing and motor-launch cruises across the lake.

But it has retained its old-world character. For the town has developed amid the ruined walls of Crusader and Turkish fortresses, whose stone has the familiar basalt colour of the region. A modest archaeological museum near the shore contains a collection of objects of antiquity found in and around Tiberias.

BETH YERACH

Some five and a half miles south of Tiberias, close to the outflow of the river Jordan from the Sea of Galilee, lies the mound of Beth Yerach, just above the water's edge. This is the site of one of the earliest cities in the country, its first settlement dating back to the end of the 4th millennium B.C., in the Early Bronze Age. It was a city of some importance in a later period, located as it was on the main highway linking Egypt with the kingdoms in the north.

Its name, which is Hebrew for "House of the Moon", and relics found on the

site, point to its having been a centre of lunar worship in Canaanite times, a widespread practice in this region in early ages.

Archaeological excavations carried out at Beth Yerach by Mr. Pesach Bar-Adon brought to light an Early Bronze Age city which, remarkably enough, had been fortified by a 25 foot thick wall. Belonging to this period were several huge grain silos, among the largest found in the Middle East. They reflect the industrious exploitation by the people at that time of the natural fertility of this area. The vessels discovered in this stratum of settlement bear witness to the highly developed pottery of the period.

This city was destroyed by the Hyksos invaders in the 18th Century B.C., to be revived many centuries later during the time of the Second Temple. After its conquest at the beginning of the 1st Century B.C. by the Hasmonean king Alexander Jannai, it became a wholly Jewish city. During the Roman occupation, a citadel was built on the site.

The most interesting of the ruins unearthed by the archaeologists and visible today are those of the very early silos, a 4th Century A.D. synagogue, a Roman bath-house also belonging to the 4th Century, and a Byzantine church built about two hundred years later.

MOUNT TABOR

Mount Tabor, six miles due east of Nazareth, squats placidly like a plump round loaf above the northern edge of the Valley of Jezreel. Rising to a height of 1850 feet, in apparent isolation, seemingly unattached to the Lower Galilee range, it figures frequently as a familiar landmark in the pages of the Old Testament.

Its best known Biblical association is with the formidable prophetess Deborah, who spurred the somewhat reluctant Barak to victorious battle with the Canaanites. "And she sent and called Barak. . . and said unto him, Hath not the Lord God of Israel commanded, saying, Go and draw toward mount Tabor, and take with thee ten thousand men of the children of Naphtali and of the children of Zebulun? And I will draw unto thee. . . Sisera, the captain of Jabin's army, with his chariots and his multitude; and I will deliver him into thine hand." (Judges IV, 6–7).

During the great revolt of the Jews against the Romans in 66 A.D., Mount Tabor was a strongpoint of the Jewish rebels in the Galilee. Some remains of their

The new Franciscan Basilica of the Transfiguration on Mount Tabor.

fortifications may still be seen on the slopes below the summit. These are the defensive works which Josephus claims to have built when he was governor of Galilee, before his defection to the Romans.

Though Tabor is not mentioned in the New Testament, Christian tradition holds it to be the scene of the Transfiguration: "And after six days Jesus taketh Peter, James, and John his brother, and bringeth them up into an high mountain apart. And was transfigured before them: and his face did shine as the sun, and his raiment was white as the light. And, behold, there appeared unto them Moses and Elias talking with him. Then answered Peter, and said unto Jesus. . . let us make here three tabernacles; one for thee, and one for Moses, and one for Elias." (Matthew XVII, 1–4).

Considered, then, by early Christians to have been the "high mountain" recorded in the Gospels, it was inevitable that the summit of Tabor should have been the site of old Christian shrines. Indeed, ruins of Byzantine churches from the 6th Century and Crusader relics from the 12th and 13th Centuries are incorporated in the new Franciscan Basilica of the Transfiguration, built in the 1920s. Close by is the Greek Orthodox Church of St. Elias (Elijah), built some ten years earlier on the remains of a Crusader structure. Since Mount Tabor was a frequent battlefield in the Crusader-Saracen fighting and changed hands several times, it was fortified by both, each often building upon or repairing the structures of the other. Relics of this work remain. The two new churches stand within the compound of the Crusader-Saracen castle. They are approached through a gate in the old Saracen wall, past the ruins of a Crusader abbey.

The summit can now be gained by a new road which climbs sharply in a series of hairpin bends. The view from the top, in all directions, is superb.

NAZARETH

Nazareth lies midway between the Mediterranean coast and the Sea of Galilee at the southernmost edge of the Lower Galilee mountain range. The city itself rests in a basin among the hills, but from the heights of its southern rim, it commands one of the most glorious views in all of Israel. Spread before it is the rich Valley of Esdraelon, scene of biblical battles, cradle of modern pioneer settlement, and today an agricultural belt of fertility and beauty. George Adam Smith made the journey through Galilee in 1880. Climbing the hills of Nazareth he looked

southwards and this is what he wrote: "Esdraelon lies before you. . . the scenes of Barak's and of Gideon's victories, the scenes of Saul's and Josiah's defeats, the scenes of the struggles for freedom in the glorious days of the Maccabees. There is Naboth's vineyard and the place of Jehu's revenge upon Jezebel; there Shunem and the house of Elisha; there Carmel and the place of Elijah's sacrifice. To the east the Valley of Jordan, with the long range of Gilead; to the west the radiance of the Great Sea, with the ships of Tarshish and the promise of the Isles. You see thirty miles in three directions. It is a map of Old Testament history."

Nazareth is the centre of the largest community of Arabs in Israel. Most of them are Christians of different denominations. The rest are Moslems. There is also a Jewish community, living, for the most part, on the outskirts of the town.

Today, Nazareth is a city of contrasts, with touches of the old and the new, of the orient and the occident. Opposite a modern church are Arab cafes, with men seated outside dressed in galabiya and kefieh and smoking the eastern pipe, the nargillah, through a bubbling bowl of rose-water, while from the open doors and windows come the insistent beat and repetitive slow trills of oriental music. Just off the main thoroughfare, with its sleek automobiles, runs the narrow cobbled lane of the old market, with its paved gutter for the donkeys bringing the field produce in panniers to the open stalls. Cheek by jowl with a new monastery is the ancient Fountain of the Virgin, reputed to have been the only well in Nazareth at the time of Jesus.

Nazareth is replete with sites venerated by Christians of all denominations. For it was here, according to the New Testament, that Joseph worked in his carpentry shop, here that Mary received the Annunciation that she was to bear Jesus, here that Jesus spent His childhood. Places touched by those lives, the cellar where the family is believed to have lived, the place where Joseph worked, the synagogue where they prayed, the well where they drew water, the site of the angelic Annunciation, have, throughout the centuries, become hallowed centres of Christian interest.

The holiest shrine, site of the Annunciation, is now marked by preparatory work for the construction of a huge basilica. It is being built above a grotto which is traditionally held to be the place where the angel Gabriel greeted Mary with "Hail, thou that art highly favoured" (Luke 1, 28) and followed it with the announcement that she would give birth to Jesus. Marking the spots where they are said to have faced each other are two granite columns, known accordingly as the "column of Gabriel" and the "column of Mary".

Sanctuaries have been built, destroyed and rebuilt on this site since the early days of Christianity. Towards the end of the 7th Century, the French Bishop Arculf, one of the first western pilgrims to leave a record of his visit to the Holy

Land, noted that there were two churches in Nazareth, one of them "built on the site of the house in which the archangel Gabriel came to the blessed Mary."

The Anglo-Saxon merchant Saewulf, the first pilgrim to follow the Crusaders and to write an account of his travels in 1102–3, found Nazareth "entirely laid waste and overthrown by the Saracens; but the place of the Annunciation. . . is indicated by a very noble monastery."

That strange British pilgrim Sir John Maundeville, whose personal narrative is interwoven with obvious, but unacknowledged, compilations from reports of earlier travellers, wrote at the beginning of the 14th Century that Gabriel's "salutation was made on the site of a great altar of a fair church that stood there formerly, but it is now all down; and they have made a little receptacle, near a pillar of that church, to receive the offerings of pilgrims. And the Saracens keep that place full dearly, for the profit they have by it; and they are very wicked and cruel Saracens, and more spiteful than in any other place, and have destroyed all the churches."

Though Maundeville's accounts are generally held to be more interesting than reliable — he was called by a noted prelate "more credulous than the most bigotted monk" — his report of demolished churches seems to have been correct. For the Burgundian knight Bertrandon de la Brocquiere, visiting Nazareth in 1432, wrote that "the place where the angel Gabriel came to announce to the Virgin Mary that she would be a mother is in a pitiful state. The church which had been built there is entirely destroyed; and of the house wherein our Lady was when the angel appeared to her, not the smallest remnant exists."

By the 17th Century, however, a new church was already standing, apparently the only one in Nazareth at the time. This we know from Henry Maundrell, the Oxford theologian noted for the sobriety and accuracy of his reports, who visited the country in 1697. Of the "columns of Mary and Gabriel", one of which seems to be suspended, with its lower portion missing, he makes the following cautious observation: "The innermost, being that of the blessed Virgin, has been broke away by the Turks, in expectation of finding treasure under it, so that eighteen inches length of it is clean gone, between the pillar and its pedestal. Nevertheless it remains erect, though by what art it is sustained I could not discern. It touches the roof above, and is probably hung upon that; unless you had rather take the friars' account of it, viz. that it is supported by a miracle!"

In a small cell adjacent to the cave with these pillars is a well preserved 6th Century mosaic with a Greek inscription. The entire Annunciation compound belongs to the Franciscans who have built a large modern monastery close to the grotto. Next to it is a small museum containing ancient relics found on the site.

The Franciscans have recently conducted archaeological excavations near the grotto with valuable results. Brought to light are the foundations of the ancient

village of Nazareth and the walls of Byzantine and mediaeval churches. It is clear from these finds that this was a residential area at the time that Jesus lived. Among the individual discoveries of archaeological interest are Byzantine mosaics, a locally fashioned Gothic capital decorated with a mask, and a beautifully sculptured torso that is believed to have depicted the angel Gabriel in the act of Annunciation. Found next to the torso, and obviously the work of the same atelier, was a capital similar to the "Nazareth Capitals" found buried nearby in excavations carried out at the beginning of this century. They are believed to have been fashioned in France some time in the 13th Century and sent to Nazareth for use in a projected new basilica which was never in fact built. They are regarded as masterpieces of French Gothic architectural sculpture.

At the northeastern end of the compound is the modern church of St. Joseph, marking the traditional site of Joseph's carpentry shop. Beneath this church is a cave scooped out of the rock which is believed to have been the dwelling place of Mary and Joseph. There is a smooth circular slab of rock in the centre of the room, left raised when the rest of the floor was levelled, to serve as a table. Sunk in the floor are pits which served as cool larders for meat and provisions and pantries for flour, oil and wine. In the wall near one of the pits, at chin level, is a small smooth ring of rock, carved out of the surface, used to belay the rope which passed through it and down to the pit to retrieve the food. Even in the heat of midsummer this cave is cool and airy.

What is called Mary's Well is a few hundred yards north of the centre of town, at the side of the main highway. Until recently, as throughout the centuries, women and children came to this well to draw their water. It was a picturesque sight which has disappeared, for Nazareth has benefited from a Government grant and is now linked to the main regional water system. The women of Nazareth might agree that a faucet in the kitchen is less romantic than carrying a pitcher to and from a well, but they infinitely prefer it.

A few yards northwest of this well stands the Greek Orthodox St. Gabriel's Church. It is their belief that this is the site where the Archangel Gabriel appeared with his Announcement to Mary.

In a market alley running west off the centre of town stands the Greek-Catholic Synagogue Church, so called because it is built on the site of an ancient structure traditionally considered to have been the synagogue frequented by Jesus.

The Mensa Christi Church is a small Franciscan chapel southwest of the town hall. It gets its name — Latin for Table of Christ — from the rock over which it is built and which is believed to have served as the table at which Jesus is said to have "taken a repast" with his disciples after the resurrection.

In terms of beauty, both of structure and of setting, the most impressive of the

Nazareth churches is that belonging to the French monks of the Salesian Order. It is called the Church of the Infant Jesus and is situated on the height above Nazareth, commanding the finest view of the city and of the country around.

For the Moslems in Nazareth, life centres round the solitary mosque, situated near the town hall, and the market place in the centre of the city.

Jutting out from the hills that form the southern rim of Nazareth, slightly east of the road to Afula, is a steep wooded mount known as the "Mount of the Leap of the Lord." This is the traditional site of the "brow of the hill" to which Jesus was led by the angry citizens of Nazareth after He had preached in the local synagogue, the hill from which "they might cast him down headlong. But he passing through the midst of them went his way, And came down to Capernaum. . ." (Luke IV, 29–31).

Four miles northeast of Nazareth on the road to Tiberias stands Kafr Kana, believed to be the village of "Cana of Galilee" where the miracle at the marriage feast of "the water that was made wine" took place. (John II). The Greek Orthodox church near the highway and the Franciscan church in the centre of the village commemorate the event. Both stand on the sites of ancient structures Beneath the Franciscan church is a fragment of a mosaic belonging probably to the 3rd or 4th Century A.D. It contains an inscription in Hebrew-Aramaic, and the possibility is strong that the early structure on this site was a synagogue.

Writers on the life of Jesus have found it difficult to recreate the Nazareth of His early years because of the silence of the Gospels concerning His youth. To this, George Adam Smith has responded that "the value of a vision of the Holy Land is that it fills in the silences." And while Nazareth in those days may well have been an obscure city, it offered a rich vantage point for the eyes of the boy Jesus and his friends who could look out from the heights of the city across Jezreel to the Samarian hills from which emerged "the road from Jerusalem, thronged annually with pilgrims, and the road from Egypt with its merchants going up and down. The Midianite caravans could be watched for miles coming up from the fords of the Jordan: and. . . the caravans from Damascus wound round the foot of the hill on which Nazareth stands. Or if the village boys climbed the northern edge of their hollow home, there was another road within sight, where the companies were still more brilliant — the highway between Acre and the Decapolis, along which legions marched, and princes swept with their retinues,

The mount of the "Leap of the Lord".

and all sorts of travellers from all countries went to and fro. The Roman ranks, the Roman eagles, the wealth of noblemen's litters and equipages cannot have been strange to the eyes of the boys of Nazareth. . ."

BETH SHE'AN

Beth She'an is the lush well-watered sub-tropical site where the Valley of Jezreel meets the Valley of the Jordan. Its fertility was bound to have attracted early settlers to this region, and archaeologists have indeed established that it was inhabited as long ago as the Chalcolithic Age in the 4th millennium B.C. Later, it found itself astride the junction of highways which linked the centres of the Middle Eastern empires. Through Beth She'an passed the trade caravans plying the Egypt-Mesopotamia route, contributing to its economic growth. Also through Beth She'an passed the troops of rival imperial armies, often leaving it devastated. It thus shared the general history of the area and of the times, a history of repetitive rise and fall. The tangible evidence of this history was unearthed during the extensive archaeological excavations carried out by an expedition of the University Museum of Pennsylvania between 1921 and 1933, directed successively by C. S. Fisher, A. Rowe and G. M. FitzGerald. The main site of their excavations was the Tell, one of the highest in the country, atop a natural hill, which was the location of the successive cities of Beth She'an, with their citadels. It is therefore called Tell el-Hosn, the "mound of the fortress". It contained eighteen levels of ancient settlement. More recently, the Israeli archaeologists Dr. Shimon Applebaum and Dr. Avraham Negev laid bare the magnificent Roman theatre and Nehemiah Zuri discovered a synagogue belonging to the 5th–6th Century A.D. Both were outside the Tell.

The earliest record of Beth She'an, like that of Hazor, appears in the 19th Century B.C. Execration Texts, and was thus clearly a city of importance in the eyes of the Egyptian rulers. It is also mentioned in the victory lists of Thutmose III, following his success at Megiddo in 1468 B.C., naming the Canaanite cities he conquered; in the 14th Century B.C. el-Amarna letters; in the 13th Century B.C. victory stelae of the pharaohs Seti I and Rameses II; and in the Papyrus Anastasi I of the same century. These records, confirmed by the excavations, showed that at this time Beth She'an was used by the Egyptians as a military base and garrison town.

Hound battling lion on sculptured basalt stele of 14th Century B.C. at Beth She'an.

It is mentioned often in the Bible, first when it was assigned to the tribe of Issachar. (It later came within the boundaries of Manasseh). (Joshua XVII, 11). Beth She'an was not taken by Joshua. It fell to the Israelites only some three hundred years later when it is believed to have been conquered by David. Shortly before that conquest, Beth She'an figured in a dramatic Biblical episode as the site where the Philistines displayed the body of the first Israelite king, Saul, who met his death on the battlefield at nearby mount Gilboa. At this time, the 11th Century B.C., pharaonic rule over the Canaanites in Beth She'an had been displaced by the Philistines. It was against them that Saul went to Gilboa to do battle — and suffered defeat. With his army in disarray, his sons killed, himself wounded by enemy archers, Saul fell upon his sword to avoid being taken alive. On the morrow, "When the Philistines came to strip the slain. . . they found Saul and his three sons fallen. . . And they cut off his head, and stripped off his armour, and sent into the land of the Philistines round about, to publish it in the house of their idols, and among the people. And they put his armour in the house of Ashtaroth: and they fastened his body to the wall of Beth-shan." (I Samuel XXXI, 8–10). The account in the Book of Chronicles records that the Philistines "put his armour in the house of their gods, and fastened his head in the temple of Dagon." (I Chronicles X, 10). During the excavations on the Tell, the archaeologists found several temples, two of them belonging to this period, one dedicated to a god and the other to a goddess. They believe these were the very "house of Ashtaroth" and "temple of Dagon" where Saul's armour and head were put on show. Evidence of the destruction of these temples a few years later suggests that this was the work of king David, who must have been anxious, in taking the city, to wipe out the structures where the remains of his predecessor had been so ig-nominiously displayed.

Israelite rule in Beth She'an lasted, with brief intervals, for some three hundred years. It then fell to the Assyrians, the Babylonians, the Persians. In Hasmonean days, it was a Hellenistic city and acquired a new name, Scythopolis, "city of the Scythians". It was now a wealthy Greek centre, the leading member of the Decapolis, the league of Ten Cities, and the only one west of the Jordan. In the Hasmonean drive to root out Hellenism, John Hyrcanus, nephew of Judah the Maccabee, conquered Beth She'an-Scythopolis in 107 B.C. It remained Jewish until the arrival of the Romans in 63 B.C. A Jewish community continued to live there, but it was now in a minority. Under the Romans, the city developed beyond the Tell, and this process was maintained during the Byzantine period. When the Moslems invaded the country in 636 A.D., Beth She'an was one of the first cities they took. It soon began to decline, and after the long Crusader inter-lude, during which it had frequently been a battlefield, it dwindled into a village. We know that in the middle ages it still had a small Jewish community and that they worshipped in a synagogue which may well have been the very one mentioned in the Talmud. For it is described by the noted Jewish writer Ashtori Haparchi, who settled in Beth She'an in the 14th Century A.D., and his description fits that in the Talmud. Beth She'an remained no more than a village right down to our own day. Only after the establishment of Israel in 1948 were efforts made to revive it.

The most important relics brought to light in the excavations of the Tell belonged to the Canaanite, Israelite, Greek, Roman and Byzantine periods. The outstanding Canaanite finds were the remains of six temples, four dating to the final period of Egyptian rule, and two — those associated with the death of Saul — to the time when Beth She'an was under Philistine authority. They were similar in structure — rectangular, built of brick, and divided into antechamber, central hall and holy of holies. The latter chamber, which held the deity, was approached by steps, at the base of which was a raised altar for sacrifices.

The archaeologists were fortunate to discover a victory stele of the pharaoh Seti I in the earliest temple. Below a relief showing the pharaoh paying homage to the sun god Ra were twenty-two lines of hieroglyphs recounting the valorous deeds of Seti in conquering "his miserable enemies". A second stele of Seti was found in an upper stratum of the site. It had been used in Byzantine times as the threshold to one of their buildings. A victory monument to Rameses II was found in the next temple. The third is believed to have been erected in the time of the pharaoh Marniptah, and the fourth in the reign of Rameses III — among the finds were his statue and a stone bearing his name. (Incidentally, today's scholars are not agreed on the specific dating given to these temples by the archaeologists who carried out the excavations). Most of the relics discovered here are now in the University Museum in Philadelphia and in the Rockefeller Museum in Jordan.

Above the Canaanite levels were remains of the Israelite period, including what may be part of a Solomonic wall. To the Hellenistic period belong the large marble pillars which may be seen on the site. They were part of a 3rd Century B.C. Greek temple which, in Byzantine times many centuries later, became the site of a large basilica — removed during the dig. The Byzantines also built a stone wall round the Tell, thus continuing the earlier tradition of using it as both citadel and shrine. The gate to this citadel was in the northwest corner, and through it lies today's track which leads to the top of the Tell. Most of the Byzantine remains, however, lie outside the mound. They include parts of the wall which surrounded the outer city, a villa, and a 6th Century A.D. monastery which has one of the finest mosaic floors found in the country.

The most impressive remains to be seen at Beth She'an are those of the Roman theatre. It is the largest, best preserved and most elaborate Roman structure in

Roman figure of marble found in theatre excavations.

Israel, with original seating accommodation for five thousand. It is built in the standard semi-circular form designed for dramatic presentations — as distinct from the circular gladiatorial amphitheatre — with the stage (proscaenium) as diameter and the public tiers (cavea) as the semi-circumference. Between cavea and proscaenium is the level semi-circular area (orchestra), which was used for seating distinguished guests. The upper part of the cavea has long crumbled into ruin, but this is hardly discernible to the casual visitor, for the fourteen tiers of the lower part are still intact, and the theatre looks complete. Also intact are the nine tunnelled exits (vomitoria) ranged round the auditorium at the level of row fourteen, and the stepped gangways which lead down to the orchestra. The huge stone stage was backed by a now ruined colonnaded structure, richly decorated with marble, statues and reliefs. Some of these were found in the debris, together with the Corinthian capitals of the columns. The theatre was built in about the year 200 A.D. Clearance of the site was carried out by the Department for Landscaping and the Preservation of Historic Sites.

The newly discovered remains of the ancient synagogue are located a few hundred yards north of the Byzantine city wall. Excellent coloured mosaics with geometric designs and themes from plant life cover the floor of the nave and aisles. The mosaic panel near the apse portrays the Ark of the Law with the seven branched candelabrum on either side. Adjoining the prayer hall were additional rooms. The archaeologists deepened the dig beneath one of them and found remains of a building which contained vessels belonging to the Hasmonean period — the 2nd and 1st Centuries B.C.

Ancient gambling dice of bone, found together with 5th Century A.D. bronze coins in Beth She'an.

BETH ALPHA

Hefzibah and Beth Alpha are adjoining kibbutzim at the foot of Mount Gilboa, lying between Afula and Beth She'an in the Valley of Jezreel. In 1928, the farmers of Hefzibah, engaged in digging an irrigation ditch, suddenly came upon part of a coloured mosaic which also bore ancient Hebrew inscriptions. They stopped work on the ditch and quickly got in touch with the Hebrew University's Professor of Archaeology, E. L. Sukenik, who promptly rushed north from Jerusalem. What he saw spurred him to conduct a comprehensive scientific dig on behalf of the University. His excavations brought to light the remains of a 6th Century A.D. synagogue, all of whose walls and pillars stood to a height of some five feet, and a mosaic floor, the most complete so far found in the country, with its manifold designs virtually intact.

The structure consisted of three main sections: an almost square court, a narrow hall and a large rectangular prayer chamber, the one leading into the other. The prayer chamber, or synagogue proper, had a semi-circular apse in its southern wall, facing Jerusalem, which originally contained the Ark of the Law and was reached by three steps. The synagogue was divided into nave and aisles by two colonnades, each of five square columns. The women's galleries were above the aisles. From the fallen stones among the debris it was clear that the original roof was gabled.

In the centre of the apse, beneath the Ark, the archaeologists found a small pit covered by stone slabs. It was no doubt used to hide the synagogue treasures, for it still contained a number of coins. Their date — plus an inscription in the floor — confirmed the dating of the construction as early 6th Century.

This synagogue was smaller than those built in the 3rd Century A.D. and the materials used were poorer, reflecting a lower standard of life than that enjoyed by the earlier Jewish settlements. We have seen, from the sequence on Bar'am, that the 3rd Century was a period of peaceful progress for the Jews of the country. And it was in that century that most of the earliest synagogues were built. With the consolidation of Christianity, however, came renewed outbreaks against the Jews which put a halt to the reconstruction of their settlements and their lives. Indeed, in the first half of the 4th Century, notably during the rule of Constantine, persecution reached the point where Jewish towns and villages were destroyed, to be resettled only some 200 years later. Again, among the first buildings to be constructed in this later period were synagogues. But they were now less imposing. They bore none of the rich decorations that adorned the older synagogues — friezes on the lintels and reliefs on the portals. The sole decoration in the 6th Century synagogues was the mosaic floor. At Beth Alpha, however, this mosaic was extraordinarily elaborate, as one can see today.

It covers the entire floor of the nave and is divided into three panels, bordered on three sides by geometric designs and representations of animals and plant life. The border on the side nearest the entrance is taken up with a Greek and Aramaic inscription, set between a lion and a bull. The inscription records that the floor was laid during the reign of the emperor Justin. It was probably Justin I, and since we know that he ruled from 518 to 527 A.D., it is possible to give an absolute date to the synagogue — a fairly rare occurrence in archaeology.

The panel near the entrance depicts the Biblical story of Abraham's would-be sacrifice of Isaac, accompanied by explanatory inscriptions taken from the Bible. Above the ram tied to a tree are the words "Behold the ram". The staying hand emerging from the heavens is captioned "Lay not" [thine hand upon the lad].

Interior of Beth Alpha synagogue, 6th Century A.D.

The names "Abraham" and "Isaac" are inscribed above their heads. The large central panel presents the signs of the Zodiac, with the symbols of the months and their names in Hebrew and Aramaic. The panel near the apse depicts the emblems of the Jewish ritual service. At the centre is an ornate Ark of the Law beneath a suspended lamp. On either side are a lion, a bird and a seven-branched candelabrum.

In subsequent repairs to part of this floor, remains of an older mosaic were found immediately beneath. They belonged to an earlier synagogue which stood upon this spot and which had been destroyed.

It may be a little confusing to the visitor that although this ancient synagogue is in the grounds of kibbutz Hefzibah, it is known by the name of the adjoining kibbutz Beth Alpha. The fact is that the site of the synagogue was part of the ancient Beth Alpha, and it was deemed appropriate to designate it by its original name.

BETH SHE'ARIM

Twelve miles southeast of the Mediterranean port of Haifa, in the gap between the Carmel range and the Lower Galilee highlands, there is a gentle sloping mound which, right up to late spring, is green with thick grass and bursting with flower. Though it lies to the immediate south of the village of Kiryat Amal and the cool wooded summer resort of Tivon, there is a quiet and serenity about this mound — as if nature were offering reverence to the souls of the departed who were buried in the extraordinary catacombs beneath. For this is the site of the necropolis of that ancient Jewish city of learning at the time of the compilation of the Mishnah, Beth She'arim.

Much was known of this important city from the wealth of literary material on the great Rabbis and scholars who walked its streets, spent their lives within its walls on a day and night study of the Torah, and were buried in its sanctified necropolis. However, not until the recent systematic excavation of this site was it definitely established as the location of Beth She'arim.

It was the accidental discovery of a tomb in 1936 that brought the archaeologist's spade to this spot. Excavations by the two Hebrew University scholars, Professors Benjamin Mazar and Nahman Avigad, who between them carried out eight seasons of digging, produced some of the most illuminating archaeological discoveries in Israel. Their work sheds new light on the lives of historic Talmudic personages and on the habits and customs of ancient times. To the visitor, the city and burial catacombs are a revelation — the fine craftsmanship of the marble work, the skill in building and tunnelling, the austere grace of the underground chambers, the marvel of the stone doors turning exquisitely on well preserved stone hinges, the bas relief ornamentation and frescoes.

Beth She'arim is most famous as the seat of the Sanhedrin, the Supreme Council of Jews, in the 2nd Century A.D., when the fulcrum of Jewish national and religious life in Palestine shifted from Judea to Galilee. It was here that the patriarch Rabbi Yehudah Ha'Nasi took up residence, here that he studied and taught, and here that he was buried. Rabbi Yehudah Ha'Nasi was the spiritual leader of Jewry at the time who bequeathed to more than seventeen centuries of Talmudic scholars his magnum opus — the codification of Judaism's oral laws, known in Hebrew as the Mishnah. He died in 220 A.D. at the age of 85.

The city itself, on top of the mound above the tombs, is believed to have been built in the 2nd Century B.C. during the period of the Hasmoneans. The historian Josephus, calling it by the Greek name Besara, refers to it as the centre of the estates owned by Berenice, daughter of Agrippa I, in "the Great Valley". Incidentally, the name Besara occurs in a Greek epigram on a marble slab found on the site.

Both from Talmudic sources and from the discoveries of both expeditions, it is clear that Beth She'arim reached its high point during the flourishing days of Rabbi Yehudah Ha'Nasi. It was destroyed in 352 A.D. during the suppression of the Jewish revolt by Gallus. There is evidence, however, that it was partly rebuilt and continued to be inhabited on a smaller scale during the Byzantine period.

The necropolis of Beth She'arim was known, from Talmudic sources, to have been the most favoured central burial place of the period for Jews both from Palestine and the Diaspora. It is believed that when the time-honoured Mount of Olives cemetery in Jerusalem became closed to Jewry after the Bar Kochba revolt in 132 A.D., the burial in Beth She'arim of Rabbi Yehuda Ha'Nasi made this the new burial centre for pious Jews. The archaeological digs revealed epigraphic evidence of this.

Diggings in the city area uncovered the remains of a large synagogue, a basilica, public buildings, dwelling houses, a glass factory and an olive press, all dating from the latter part of the 2nd to the middle of the 4th Century A.D. Most important is the large synagogue. It is of the intermediate Palestinian type, not unlike the ancient synagogue at Capernaum. Marble slabs with ornamental reliefs and inscriptions covered the plastered walls of the prayer hall. From a hoard of 1200 coins found in the cinders of one of the rooms in an adjacent

Lions carved on sarcophagus in Beth She'arim catacombs.

building, and from other relics in the synagogue area, it is clear that this site was destroyed shortly after 350 A.D.

It is, however, the necropolis of Beth She'arim that offers the most archaeological interest. Funerary chambers, catacombs and the general subterranean architecture are unique. Here was a cemetery cut deep in the rock on the hill slopes, designed as a palatial underground city of the lifeless, approached by courtyards, corridors and steps, complete with vaulted halls and chambers ornamented with bas relief and fresco. To stand before these man-made catacombs is to stand on the threshold of two worlds, the world of the living and the world of the dead.

At the entrance to each catacomb is an open courtyard, formed by slicing out a segment of the hillside. Access to the courts from the newly built road which skirts the mound is direct. Cut in the three walls of the rock round each courtyard are apertures closed by stone doors. These doorways give access to the halls and burial chambers of the catacombs. The doors, which are in an excellent state of preservation, are made of a single stone slab, sculptured to give the appearance of panelled wood. Two of the openings have double doors.

Each catacomb consists of a series of halls and side chambers. Each hall is entered by one of the stone doors in the courtyard. Running off the sides of these long halls, through arched openings, are the burial chambers. This is the standard pattern in all but two of Beth She'arim's catacombs, where there are no side chambers, only large halls. Almost 300 burial inscriptions have so far been found, in Hebrew, Greek, Aramaic and Palmyrene (a dialect of Palmyra, now in Syria). Some of the catacombs have plain walls. Others have a profusion of ornamental reliefs and decorative markings. The engravings, graffiti, reliefs and paintings are primitive. Religious Jewish symbols are the most common motifs and are carried out in varying techniques, from the bold relief to the light brush painting and the crude scratch. Frequent in all catacombs are the seven-branched candelabrum, the Ark of the Law, the ram's horn, the palm branch and citron. But there are also representations of secular subjects, ships, animals, human figures, geometric designs, plants and fruit. Sometimes there is a pictorial representation of a Biblical episode, like Daniel in the lions' den or Noah in the ark. Sometimes the subject is topical, like a Roman legionary and gladiators, or mythological, like the relief on a marble sarcophagus of Leda and the swan.

No marking has so far been found to establish the tomb of Rabbi Yehudah Ha'Nasi. But there is one catacomb, more ornate than the rest, which has an elaborate facade of three great arches resting on pillars with moulded capitals and bases. Above the arched facade is a flight of steps, wide and shallow, leading to a wall with a curved niche flanked by two rectangular columns. It was clearly designed as a decorative adornment to the sepulchre beneath, within which were found two Hebrew inscriptions. One reads "This is (the tomb) of Rabbi

Gamaliel". The other reads simply "Rabbi Simeon". Now Rabbis Simeon and Gamaliel were the names of the two sons of Rabbi Yehudah Ha'Nasi. The supposition was therefore strong that this was indeed their family vault. Further excavations, however, have shown that this tomb belongs to a somewhat later period and the location of Rabbi Yehudah's burial place is still unknown.

MEGIDDO

Megiddo, strategic centre in Biblical and earlier ages, is today a site of rich archaeological interest. It lies 22 miles southeast of Haifa, and the modern highway which links it to that Mediterranean port city skirts the Carmel range and the hills of Samaria. With their rugged slopes as a backdrop, Megiddo commands, to the immediate north and east, the fruitful Valley of Jezreel, also known as Esdraelon, in which mighty Biblical battles were fought. In those times, this valley was green and fertile. Then came the long centuries of decline. Today, revived by the pioneers of Israel, it is a tapestry of vineyards and orchards, and fields of wheat and corn, barley, alfalfa and clover; and its main colour themes are again emerald and gold. Twelve miles to the north, across the valley, are the heights which enclose Nazareth; a little to the east is Mount Tabor, and beyond, in the distant northeast, seventy miles away, looms the snow-capped peak of Mount Hermon. This is the panorama that greets the visitor to the Hill of Megiddo.

It lies at the head of a mountain pass, guarding access to the north from the coastal plain. This gave it high strategic value throughout history. Megiddo commanded the great trunk road from Egypt in the south to Mesopotamia and Syria in the north, the celebrated Via Maris. It also guarded the east-west road across Jezreel. The key to northern Israel, it was an object of fortification by its occupiers, and of attack by contending empires, through the ages — right up to the First World War in this century. The Egyptians, Canaanites, Philistines, Israelites, Assyrians, Persians, Greeks and Romans were the principal dramatis personae in the bitter battles fought here in ancient times. In 1918, the Allied Armies under Allenby entered northern Palestine through the Megiddo Pass to drive out the Turkish forces, and the British commander, elevated to the peerage, took as his title Viscount Allenby of Megiddo.

Megiddo was first excavated by the German archaeologist G. Schumacher, who carried out a dig almost single-handed in 1903–5. In 1925, the Oriental Institute

Ivory openwork plaque, found at Megiddo, 1350–1150 B.C.

Model of reconstructed Israelite city of Megiddo.

of the University of Chicago started large-scale excavations under the direction of C. S. Fisher, P. L. O. Guy and G. Loud. The expedition was financed by the Rockefeller family, and it continued its highly successful scientific work up to the outbreak of war in 1939. Since then, the mound was neglected, its matchless relics disappearing under weed and bramble. In 1958, the Department for Landscaping and the Preservation of Historic Sites of the Israel Government began work on the clearance and restoration of the site.

The first mention of Megiddo occurs in Egyptian writngs as the scene of attack by the Egyptian pharaoh Thutmose III in the year 1468 B.C. This Battle of Megiddo, in which the king of Kadesh and his allies were defeated by Thutmose, is described in hieroglyphics found in Egyptian temples. Nearly thirty years later, there is a description of the campaign undertaken by pharaoh Amenhotep II, son of Thutmose, in which he passed through the Sharon Plain, rested "in the vicinity of Megiddo" and there sat in judgment on the "rebellious princes".
Megiddo is also mentioned in one of the Taanach Letters, written in Accadian cuneiform, discovered at the beginning of this century. Taanach is a few miles southeast of Megiddo. The writer is an Egyptian general who urges an apparently reluctant king of Taanach to pay his tribute. "May Baal protect you," writes the general. "Send me your charioteers and horses, presents for me, and send all your prisoners. Send them tomorrow to Megiddo".
Megiddo is referred to in several of the cuneiform tablets that make up the Tell el-Amarna Letters, written to the Egyptian Court by Canaanite vassals. Much is learnt of conditions in the Megiddo city during the 14th century B.C. from the six letters by Biridiya, king of Megiddo, to pharaoh Amenhotep IV, in which he fulsomely affirms his loyalty, underlines his concern for the pharaoh's interests, recalls the scrupulous transmission of his tribute from the harvest of the fields, but warns that these taxes are seriously jeopardised by the depredations of his marauding neighbours. He begs Amenhotep to send a defence contingent of 100 men to save "your city", the city of Megiddo.

There is frequent mention of Megiddo in the Bible. The first occurs in Joshua. Chapter XII lists "... the kings of the land, which the Children of Israel smote..." One of them is "the king of Megiddo..." (XII, 21). In Judges (v, 19), the song of Deborah, which follows the description of the defeat of the Canaanite army under Sisera by the prophetess and Barak, says "The kings came and fought, then fought the kings of Canaan in Taanach by the waters of Megiddo..."
In the 10th Century B.C., king Solomon rebuilt and fortified Megiddo, financing its construction with a special levy, as is recorded in the First Book of Kings (IX, 15): "And this is the reason of the levy which king Solomon raised; for to

Megiddo, aerial view.

build the house of the Lord, and his own house, and Millo, and the wall of Jerusalem, and Hazor, and Megiddo, and Gezer." It became one of the Solomonic "cities for chariots", complete with elaborate stables.

In the 9th Century B.C., Ahaziah, king of Judah, ". . . fled to Megiddo, and died there", as we are told in the Second Book of Kings (IX, 27).

In the year 609 B.C., the noble king of Judah, Josiah, fell in battle at Megiddo against the invading Egyptians. "And his servants carried him to Jerusalem, and buried him in his own sepulchre". (II Kings XXIII, 30).

Its frequency as a scene of battle made Megiddo symbolic of warfare. In the New Testament book, Revelation, Megiddo is envisioned as the site of the last great battle to be fought at the end of time. "For they are the spirits of devils working miracles, which go forth unto the kings of the earth and of the whole world, to gather them to the battle of that great day of God Almighty. . . And he gathered them together into a place called in the Hebrew tongue Armageddon". (XVI, 14, 16). Armageddon is a corruption of Har Megiddon, Hebrew for the Hill of Megiddo.

The excavations at Megiddo uncovered twenty super-imposed cities, the first, at the lowest stratum, dating back to the Chalcolithic period in the 4th millennium, and the last belonging to the 4th Century B.C. Thereafter, the site seems to have been abandoned in favour of a fortress closer to the Megiddo Pass. Each of the buried cities was represented by a distinct layer of ruins and other remains of occupation. Some of them were removed as soon as they were recorded and photographed, to make way for the next stratum beneath. However, the important structural relics of earlier ages have been left on the site and may be seen today. These belong chiefly to the 9th Century B.C. city, with its unique water-system, to the Solomonic city of the 10th Century B.C., to the city gate used from the 16th to the 12th Centuries B.C., to the Hyksos cities of the 18th–16th Centuries B.C., and to the early Canaanite cities of the 3rd millennium B.C.

The building at the entrance to Megiddo, formerly the headquarters of the Rockefeller expedition, is now the Megiddo Museum. A few yards beyond, along the path towards the northern slope of the mound, is an ancient roadway which was the original main approach to the city. It was laid down during the reign of king David. A later road of rubble, built above it in Solomon's time, was removed during the excavations. To the left are the remains of the foundations of the heavy gate built by king Solomon, with its basalt door-sockets, originally lined with iron. In plan and style, this gate is similar to those in the two other Solomonic "chariot cities", Hazor and Gezer, and all three show the same architec-

97

tural hand. It has a tower at each side of the entrance, and the gatehouse for the guards consists of six chambers, three on each side of the entrance. Biblical scholars, after studying the archaeological reports of the discovery of the Solomonic gates in Gezer and Megiddo, were quick to notice that their description perfectly fits the eloquent detailing of the eastern wall of the Temple in the vision of the Prophet Ezekiel: "Then came he unto the gate which looketh towards the east, and went up the stairs thereof, and measured the threshold of the gate... And the little chambers of the gate eastward were three on this side, and three on that side..." (Ezekiel XL, 6–10). Ezekiel was familiar with the ruins of the Temple in Jerusalem, and he was clearly describing in his vision a gate whose foundations he had actually seen, and probably measured. It is evident that the eastern gate of the Temple was designed by the same Solomonic architect who had constructed the gates of Megiddo, Gezer and Hazor.

To the right are the remains of an earlier gate, at a lower level, which served the cities from the 16th to the 12th centuries. Further to the right are the remains of an even older gate, belonging to the Hyksos period and dating back to the 18th Century B.C. This gate lies at the bottom of a deep archaeologist's "cut" which runs down through several strata, the lowest belonging to the 18th and the uppermost to the 16th Century. This upper level contains several small mud and stone dwellings typical of the late Hyksos period. The lowest stratum contains a well-preserved cobbled street lined by very thick walls made of mud bricks.

The remains of the wall to the east of the gate were attributed by archaeologists until recently to Solomon. The ruins show it to have been a well-built structure erected on a foundation of stone, sturdy and solid, whose outer surface was marked by salients and recesses. The salients served as a kind of bastion.

To the Israeli archaeologist Dr. Yigael Yadin, the attribution of such a wall to the Solomonic period did not seem feasible. The Solomonic gates in Hazor, which he had excavated, and in Gezer, which had been explored earlier, were linked to a casemate wall. This type of wall was not solid but contained hollow chambers between its inner and outer surfaces. It seemed odd that Solomon should have called for another type of wall for Megiddo, when presumably it was intended as a fortification against the same kind of battering ram with which potential enemies at that time could threaten his other cities. Moreover, the solid "salients and recesses" type of wall was a feature of the period which followed Solomon.

Prodded by these intriguing doubts, Yadin carried out a brief experimental dig at Megiddo in 1961. It produced the remarkable discovery of casemate ruins beneath the solid wall, linked to the Solomonic gate. Solomon's fortification network at Megiddo was thus the same as that at Hazor and Gezer.

Slightly northwest of Solomon's gate are the remains of the 16th century B.C. Canaanite wall. Nearby is the site of the palaces of the Canaanite kings, each

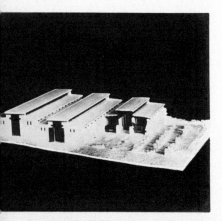

Model of partially restored Megiddo stables.

Remains of dwelling house in period of Israelite Kingdom.

built on the foundations of the earlier structure. It was in one of these palaces, later removed by the archaeologists to expose lower strata, that the great treasure of carved ivories was found, belonging to the 13th and 12th Centuries. These are known as the Megiddo Ivories, and are among the finest collection of their kind in the world. Photographs of the most outstanding of these ivory trinkets are on display in the Megiddo Museum.

The Museum also contains a replica of the 8th Century "Megiddo Seal". This is a reproduction of a lion with the Hebrew inscription "Belonging to Shema servant of Jeroboam". Nothing is known of Shema, but he is presumed to have been the governor of Megiddo at the time of the Israel king, Jeroboam II, who reigned from 786 to 746 B.C. This, then, was Shema's Seal, found in a beautiful state of preservation during the Schumacher excavation.

The western edge of the mound contains one of the most remarkable examples of the skilled engineering of ancient days — the ingenious water system. Until recently, scholars attributed its date to the 12th Century B.C., but following the Yadin excavation in 1961, it is now known to be post-Solomonic, probably 9th Century B.C. This system ensured a regular supply of fresh water for the inhabitants of Megiddo from springs outside the city walls, even during siege, and it is still well preserved after some two thousand eight hundred years.

The ancient engineers sunk a large shaft into the ground to a depth of 120 feet. From the bottom of the shaft, a tunnel was cut through the rock for a distance of 215 feet to a spring outside the city. The spring opening was hidden by a wall camouflaged by a covering of earth, and thus went unnoticed by besieging forces. There are signs that the tunnel was bored by two working parties operating from each end. It says much for their skill that when they met in the middle, they were not out more than a few inches in height and only two feet laterally. In the recent restoration of the site, a staircase was installed in the shaft and electric lighting in the tunnel, so that the whole underground system can be explored with ease.

At the southern part of the mound are the ruins of stables. Until 1961, these were believed to have been the stables of Solomon, but they are now known to be of somewhat later date, probably 9th Century B.C. They are identical in plan to another set of stables unearthed by the archaeologists near the city gate and removed by them after excavation. They comprised five parallel sheds, each containing twenty-two stalls in parallel rows of eleven. In each stall was a stone pillar to which the horses were tethered. The pillars also helped to support the roof. Near each pillar was a manger, cut out of solid limestone.

A little to the east of the stable area, also at the southern edge of the mound, are the remains of a large building surrounded by a wall, giving the impression of a

Female figurine of ivory, from the treasury in the palace at Megiddo, 1350–1150 B.C.

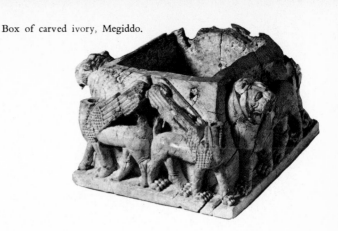

Box of carved ivory, Megiddo.

fort within a fort. This is believed to have served as the residence of the governor of Megiddo.

In the centre of the mound are the remains of a large silo belonging to the 8th Century. It is shaped like an inverted cone with blunted nose. Two sets of steps in the wall of the silo, facing each other, lead down into the interior.

Southeast of the silo is a group of pillars looking not unlike the hitching posts of the stable. They are, in fact, the structural pillars of a large building erected before the 10th Century. Nearby are the ruins of another public building of the same period.

The remaining relics of importance — and the oldest — are at the eastern end of the Megiddo mound. These are the three Canaanite temples belonging to the 2nd millennium B.C. Each consisted of a large chamber with an altar at the southern side, flanked by two carved pillar bases. Nearby is a porch giving on to the street. Archaeologically, the most interesting altar is in the southeast temple. It is a circular "high place" built of stone, with steps leading up to it. This site may be called the "temple compound" of Megiddo, for it was the traditional location of its shrines. The first is believed to have been established here at the end of the 4th millennium B.C., and later temples were built on the ruins of earlier ones throughout the entire Canaanite period.

Today's restoration enables the modern visitor to step back into antiquity and recapture the pattern of life in fortified Megiddo — Megiddo of the Bible.

MONTFORT

The crusader Castle of Montfort is the most spectacular ruin in western Galilee, rising from the summit of a dominating hill above a winding brook. It lies nine miles due east, as the crow flies, from the stretch of Mediterranean coast between Nahariya and Rosh Hanikra on the Lebanese border. For humans, the approach is more tortuous, and more difficult, for the planned access road has not yet been built; but the effort is highly rewarding.

From Eilon, a village along the northern border road seven miles from the coast, Montfort can be reached on foot across two miles of hills and valleys. It can be gained from the south by walking along the dirt track which shoots off from Me'iliya, three miles away, on the main highway from Nahariya to Safad. To the intrepid jeep rider there is a third route. This lies along the bumpy bank of

the Keziv stream that runs through a wooded glen right to the foot of the fortress –
a distance of five miles from the Matsuba-Kabri link road. Midway along this
winding route, one suddenly comes upon the jagged outlines of the castle ruins
set in mystic grandeur against the sky.

The main structures of the castle were built by the Crusader Order of Templars.
The exact date is not known, but it was probably at the end of the 12th Century
A.D. or the beginning of the 13th. The castle was enlarged by the Order of
Teutonic Knights some years later, probably in the 1230's.

The religious-military Orders were proud and powerful organisations which
had developed, paradoxically, from a humble and humane service — care of the
sick. When the merchants of Amalfi endowed the Hospital of St. John, near the
Church of the Holy Sepulchre in Jerusalem, for the benefit of Christian pilgrims,
a small group of Crusader knights resolved to undertake the care of these patients.
Later, they added to these duties the task of defending the Christian faith — by
fighting non-believers — and created a military Order attached to the hospital.
It thus became known as the Order of Hospitalers, though its official title was
the Order of the Knights of St. John of Jerusalem. It assumed the profession of
arms in 1120, and its military tasks soon outgrew its former medical mission.
But it continued to respect its hospital duties. These were carried out by "serving
brothers", while the fighting was done by warrior-knights.

A little later, another small group of knights who had joined the First Crusade,
some of whom had also served in the Hospital of St. John, took upon themselves
the safeguarding of pilgrims on their way from Jaffa to Jerusalem. Soon, they too
extended their scope to embrace "defence of the faith", engaging in purely
military activities, unfettered by the calls of medical welfare. They were particularly active after 1123. Their headquarters were established in the Dome of the
Rock compound, on the site of the Temple of Solomon, and so their organisation
became known as the Order of Templars.

These two Orders later took over the garrisoning and policing of the entire
country under Crusader rule and built a chain of castles at strategic locations
which were among the most imposing examples of feudal fortification. They
acquired much land round these castles and the knights in fact became feudal
lords, owing allegiance not to the Crusader king in Jerusalem but directly to the
Pope, and drawing powerful financial help from the European kingdoms. Their
pattern of living accorded ill with their professed ideals of Christianity. They
were cruel, dissolute and quarrelsome, though they could fight with valour if not
always with vigilance — as was shown in their bloody defeat at the Horns of
Hattin. Gibbon put it incomparably in his *Decline and Fall of the Roman Empire*:
"But in their most dissolute period the knights of the hospital and temple main-

tained their fearless and fanatic character: they neglected to live, but they were prepared to die, in the service of Christ. . ."

After the fall of Jerusalem to Saladin in 1187, a third Order was established, this time by the German Crusaders. It was called the Order of Teutonic Knights. Unlike the two older Orders, which had an international, though predominantly French, membership, the Teutonic Order received into its ranks only knights from German speaking countries. It was organised and it developed rapidly after the Third Crusade — which came out soon after the loss of Jerusalem — when German merchants from Lubeck and Bremen founded a hospital for their compatriots in Acre. The Teutonic Order followed the Hospitalers in combining medical care with military duties. Its headquarters, established first in Acre, were later transferred to Montfort. This Order never reached the importance of the earlier two, since it was founded at a period when the Crusader kingdom was already in decline. Operating for the most part in western Galilee, it erected or enlarged several castles. The most distinguished was Montfort.

The original Montfort was constructed as a defensive outpost to protect the large estate centred on the Chateau du Roi — the King's Castle — at Me'iliya. It was therefore also known as Castellum Novum Regis — the King's New Castle. In 1229 it was sold by the Templars to the Teutonic Order, who were looking for a new headquarters' site. Life for them in Acre, with the bitter rivalry between the Orders, had become too frustrating. With funds received largely from the Duke of Austria, the German knights undertook a large rebuilding programme to enable the castle to meet new needs. For it now had to house the treasury of the Order, its archive and the Residence of the Master. The new owners Germanised the name Montfort, in literal translation, to Starkenberg.

In 1266, the fortress was beseiged by the Mameluke sultan Baibars, but it held out successfully. Five years later, Baibars attacked again, this time penetrating the southern section of the wall and reaching the courtyard. The effects of the undermining of this wall may be seen on the site today. The Crusaders retired to the great keep, but soon capitulated. The sultan ordered the destruction of the wall and the burning of all wooden buildings. But he apparently spared the lives of the enemy survivors and allowed them to leave, taking with them the archive of the Order. This was transferred to Acre and later to Germany. It remains one of the few Crusader archives to have been preserved in its entirety, and is most informative on the history and geography of Galilee during that period. The castle was never again rebuilt.

Archaeological excavations were carried out at Montfort in 1926 by an expedition from the New York Metropolitan Museum of Art. They established that the hill had been settled and fortified in ancient times, probably during the period of the Israelite kings and certainly in the days of Roman rule. Some of the huge stones

in the Crusader buildings came in fact from Roman ruins, and some from an even earlier date. Roman coins and vessels were also unearthed in the castle compound. They are on display in the Metropolitan Museum, together with the 13th Century Crusader weapons and armour found in the castle smithy.

The castle covers an east to west strip on the summit of a hill which offered two main natural defence features — a steep northern slope which runs down 600 feet to the Keziv stream, and a steep southern slope which ends in a ravine. The western gradient is gentle, and this determined the construction of the fortress in terrace style which provided defence in depth. The most vulnerable side was the eastern, for here a narrow spur linked the summit to the adjoining high ground in this hilly region. To overcome such weakness, the Crusaders cut a deep moat on this side which "severed" the spur and gave total isolation to the mount. On the castle side of the moat they built a huge stone wall, and behind it they erected a formidable tower, or keep, which also gave protection to the main gate immediately below, on the southern slope. This keep, sometimes referred to as the Great Tower, was the castle's strongest bastion.

Encircling the entire hill was the outer wall of the fort — now no longer standing. Closer to the buildings was a 1500 foot long inner wall which was strengthened by a series of towers, complete with windows and embrasures, constructed at fixed intervals with complementary fields of fire to leave no approach area uncovered. The western section of this wall, still preserved, is curved, suiting the contour of the hill and offering a wider angle of fire to its tower.

The structural plan of the castle, from east to west, was as follows: moat, wall, keep, courtyard, knights' dwelling quarters, workshop and kitchen, chapel, ceremonial hall, residence of the Master of the Order and the curved part of the inner wall. These buildings formed a mass of masonry covering an area of 450 by 80 feet and rising to a height of 90 feet above the summit.

At the foot of the northern slope of the hill, outside the castle proper, is another Crusader building in a good state of preservation. It has two storeys and it served as the central farm building of the castle estate, the ground floor being used as stables for draft animals and storehouses for equipment and farm produce. The upper storey has a beautifully vaulted roof. This building also protected the approaches to the source of water — the Keziv stream. The water was carried to the top by mule and stored in large cisterns cut in the rock within the castle compound. In the bed of the stream are ruins of small dams and channels used to divert the water to mills on the banks of the brook.

At the side of the building is a broad dirt path which spirals its way up the hill to the summit, skirting old oak trees that rise from the southern ravine. At one

Leaf-motif carved on Crusader stone found at Montfort.

Fish symbol on stone, found at Montfort.

point, the cleft is spanned by a small Crusader bridge which is joined by another broad path running in from Me'iliya — the southern approach. Keeping to the path that clings to the hill, one soon reaches part of the retaining wall of the buildings above, the edge of the castle garden, and the outside of one of the towers that served as bastions to the inner wall. This tower still stands to a height of some 55 feet and its window apertures and embrasures are intact. To the immediate east of this tower are two chambers with arched roofs which were the cellars of the Master's residence. Part of a large stone arch which now lies on the cellar floor comes from the collapsed roof of the hall above it.

A short steep path from the cellars leads to the main level of the castle. The first ruin to be reached is now but an echo of what was the antechamber to the ceremonial hall attached to the Master's residence. The greater part of its walls and a section of the floor have long crumbled and rolled down the hillside. The ceremonial hall is now also very much ruined, though one can gauge its former strength and magnificence by the relics which still stand. It was a square chamber, with sides 60 feet long and walls 6 feet thick. From the octagonal pillar in the centre sprang the eight ribs of the vaulted ceiling. Of the wall pillars, only some of the bases remain. Adjoining this hall to the west was the main wing of the Master's palace, the best preserved of the castle ruins, and the rooms housing the treasury and archive. The residence gave on to the castle garden which extended down to the curved part of the inner wall.

On the other side of the ceremonial hall was the rectangular chapel. Fragments of stained glass were found here during the excavations, parts of the original decorative windows set in the southern wall. East of the chapel were the kitchen of the garrison and the two large dwelling halls of the knights. In the kitchen the archaeologists found an array of large earthenware vessels used for provisions; and in one corner, set aside no doubt for the storage and preparation of drugs, they found pieces of bottles and flasks and parts of a pestle and mortar.

The small room at the side of the kitchen was the castle smithy. It was here that the archaeologists discovered bars of iron, tools, sections of armour and broken weapons. They included crucibles, hammers and chisels; fragments of chain mail, part of a visor, scales of an armoured jacket and forty pieces of armour; arrow-heads, darts, lances and spikes, all lying in a bed of charcoal. Also close to the kitchen is a wine press with its treading pit and fermentation vat. At the side of the smithy are steps which lead to the roof.

East of the domestic quarters is the stone-paved courtyard, originally the main entrance court to the fortress, to which a stone path led from the castle gate. Large steps cut in the rock lead from the court to the keep.

This keep was a square structure, erected on the highest point of the hill, and dominating the entire castle area. It was built largely of massive stones, some of

Crusader Castle Judin at Yehiam.

them 9 feet long, taken from the ruins of more ancient fortifications. It was here that the excavators found Roman coins. In the floor of this great tower is a huge water cistern scooped out of the rock. To its east is the moat, now the repository of debris from the destroyed stone wall which stood between moat and keep.

Montfort is a site of considerable Crusader interest. It is also one of the beauty spots of the country.

Some six miles due south of Montfort are the remains of another Crusader castle. This was Castle Judin, built by the Templars at the end of the 12th Century. This, too, passed into the hands of the Teutonic Knights — twenty-one years before they took over their new headquarters' fortress. It was destroyed by Baibars in 1265, and it was after this that he laid his first and unsuccessful siege against Montfort.

What was left of that destruction was incorporated five hundred years later in the palatial stronghold built in the 1760's by the powerful Sheikh Tahar al Amr. The Crusader remains include the two lower storeys of the large eastern tower of the castle, parts of another tower, and halls with vaulted ceilings. Sections of the walls still standing contain embrasures.

The ruins adjoin kibbutz Yehiam.

ACRE

Acre is one of the oldest cities in the world, known in Biblical times as Accho. It lies on the coast in northern Israel at the tip of a broad crescent bay that sweeps southwards to Haifa, nine miles away. It enjoys, in the words of an early traveller to the Holy Land, "all possible advantages of both sea and land. On its north and east sides, it is compassed with a spacious and fertile plain; on the west, it is washed by the Mediterranean Sea; and to its South is a large bay, extending from the city as far as mount Carmel." Today, as you approach Acre across the flat plain, its bubble domes and tall minarets appear to float unreal above the indigo blue of the sea, and all that seems to tie the city down are the sturdy palm trees, the stone ramparts left by the Crusaders and the ruined buildings of the Turkish period. These Crusader and Turkish ruins are the only remaining signposts of Acre's eventful and stirring history. And they give the city its special character, part mediaeval, part Ottoman. In the old quarter, where the buildings are crowded together along narrow streets and alleys, the population is as mixed as ever —

Christian Arabs whose fair hair and blue eyes are traceable to Crusader times, dark-skinned Moslem families, Druzes, Bahais, and thousands of Jewish immigrants from many lands who have picked up the broken threads of Jewish settlement woven into the life of Acre at different periods throughout the last three thousand years.

Acre is mentioned in the Bible as part of the territory assigned as a heritage to the tribe of Asher. But, as recorded in the Book of Judges, it was not taken at the time of the major conquest of Canaan. In the days of king Solomon, Acre is believed to have been a transit city for his Cilician imported horses.

In the New Testament, Acre is referred to by the name given to it in the 3rd Century B.C. — Ptolemais, the Ptolemais of Paul referred to in The Acts. (XXI, 7).

Its commercial value as a natural port and its strategic importance as a convenient point of entry into Palestine made Acre a coveted target for would-be conquerors throughout history. Its sheltered harbour served merchant vessels engaged in the levant trade, turning Acre into a flourishing entrepot centre. The same favourable naval facilities and the ease of approach from Acre to the interior tempted sea-borne invaders of the country to choose it as the site of assault. Invaders by land, from north or south, were attracted both by Acre's coastal advantages and by its commanding position astride the narrow pass of the Ladder of Tyre. But its excellent defensive position enabled Acre to hold out against most of its assailants.

The most spectacular attack in Acre's history which succeeded was the land and sea assault of the Crusaders at the start of the 12th Century A.D. The most spectacular attack which failed was the landward attempt by Napoleon 700 years later.

The Crusaders entered Palestine at the end of the 11th Century through Byzantium, Antioch (now Turkey), and Tripoli (now Lebanon), and marched on Jerusalem which they captured in 1099.

They had aimed to take some of the coastal cities, including Acre, en route, but gave up the idea. Jerusalem was their principal objective and they wasted little time and men on side skirmishes, though once established in Jerusalem, they resolved to secure the sea ports. In the first years of the 12th Century, after receiving the promised help from fleets based on Italy, they began a systematic cleaning up of the coast. Jaffa had been the only coastal city in Crusader hands. Now, in 1104, the army of Baldwin I, Crusader king of Jerusalem, with the help of the Genoese fleet, successfully forced the capitulation of Acre. Thus began the Crusader association with the city. Under the Crusaders, Acre revived as an important commercial centre.

In 1187, the Saracens under the Kurd, Salah ed-Din, known to the western world as Saladin, fresh from their decisive victory over the Crusaders at the Battle of Hattin, took Acre. But two years later, it was put under siege by the very Crusader baron who had through inexperience led his forces to disaster at Hattin— Guy de Lusignan, successor to his brother-in-law, Baldwin IV, as king of Jerusalem. He had been released from captivity in a chivalrous gesture by Saladin. While the siege was still in progress, he was joined by king Philip Augustus of France and the celebrated king of England, Richard Coeur de Lion. But it was not until 1191 that Acre fell, the glory of victory being credited by some history books to king Richard alone. A year later, after unsuccessful Crusader efforts to recapture Jerusalem, peace with the Moslems was made on the basis of the status quo and Acre became the Crusader capital, remaining their most important city until its capture by the Mameluke al-Malik al-Ashraf Khalil a hundred years later. The fall of Acre in 1291 put an end to Crusader rule in the country. Most of the Crusader remains in Acre today date from the period when it was their capital.

With the departure of the Crusaders, Acre was systematically destroyed, to prevent the Europeans from regaining a foothold. In 1775, Ahmed al-Jazzar Pasha became the Turkish High Commissioner in the Acre Pashalik. He was a vigorous governor, determined to restore Acre to its former position as a commerical centre, and to remodel it on the pattern of Constantinople. It was he who built the existing walls, the bath-house, and the beautiful mosque which are to this day the most graceful structures in the city.

In 1799, Napoleon tried to take Acre. It became the scene of the greatest setback in his entire eastern campaign. In May of the previous year, he and his army had sailed from Toulon for a secret destination. Two months later he had secured control of all Egypt. Then came a grave blow which was to have its effect on his later siege of Acre. His fleet was destroyed by Britain's Admiral Nelson at the Battle of the Nile. He remained in Egypt until mid-winter — incidentally engaging in several scientific and archaeological projects — and then moved into Palestine, sweeping up the coast, past El Arish and Jaffa and moving northwards until he encamped outside Acre. From Jaffa he had sent his siege guns northwards by sea, timing his assault on Acre with their arrival. But they never got there. A British naval squadron under Sir Sydney Smith spotted them, and with no French fleet to protect them, they were captured. Smith then sped to Acre and together with Ahmed al-Jazzar, his Jewish adviser Haim Farhi, and a brilliant French Royalist — anti-revolutionary — engineer, Colonel Phelippeaux, built up the defences of the city. Deprived of his heavy artillery, Napoleon's first assaults failed. And he was forced to resort to lengthy but vigorous siege

tactics, while at the same time fighting off harassing attacks on his flank by newly assembled Turkish forces from Damascus who were beaten back at Tabor. Some weeks later, three French frigates arrived bringing new siege guns. The assaults were renewed, and Smith's despatches home at the time revealed his fears that Acre would fall. But the defences held. And the arrival of a Turkish fleet from Rhodes at the beginning of May neutralised the French frigates. By the middle of the month, his plans frustrated, Napoleon decided to call a halt to the campaign. On the 18th May, after almost two months of siege, he gave the order to retreat. Within two days there was hardly a trace of his camp. By the beginning of June he had recrossed the frontier into Egypt. Two months later he set sail secretly for Europe, leaving behind his dreams of an eastern empire.

In 1832, Ibrahim Pasha of Egypt drove the Turks from Acre and established his rule in the city. Eight years later he was forced to withdraw when the fleets of Turkey's European allies bombarded Acre and restored Turkish authority.

Over the next few decades Acre again went into decline, and gradually gave way in importance as a port to neighbouring Haifa. With the British capture of Palestine in 1918, Haifa became the headquarters of the northern district, and Acre struggled on as an unimportant, though charming, fishing village. It became a battle-ground once again in May 1948 during Israel's War of Liberation, falling to Israel's forces on 17 May, two days after the proclamation of the State.

Entering Acre from the main Haifa road, you skirt the old quarter to reach the coast along which runs a broad Turkish rampart built to guard the city from coastal attack. A few hundred yards to the south, steps lead to an opening in this sea-wall and give on to what looks like a bastion jutting out over the water. It is in fact a semi-circular artillery platform with embrasures in the parapet for the gun barrels which commanded a 180 degrees field of fire against attacking vessels. The cannon are still there, including some captured from the French by Sydney Smith during the Napoleonic siege.

Across the road from the sea-wall is the wall enclosing the old city. Immediately inside is the Citadel, an 18th Century Turkish structure built on 13th Century Crusader foundations. Before 1948 it was used as the central prison of the British administration, and during the period of active resistance, after the second world war, many of the underground Jewish fighters were confined here. Some went to their death in the execution chamber of this very building.

Beneath the citadel is a hall which, though still known as the Crypt of St. John, is now believed to have been the refectory of the Hospitalers' palace. It is the most important Crusader site in the whole of Acre, and can now be reached by an

The mosque of al-Jazzar, Acre.

independent entrance in the nearby lane. Current restorations have removed the debris of centuries to reveal a fine vaulted hall, magnificently proportioned, with sculptured decorations on the ceiling.

Slightly southeast of the citadel is the impressive Mosque of Al-Jazzar. The hall of worship is approached through marble-columned arcades which enclose a large sunny square court built over Crusader vaults. It is a court of contemplation, of quiet charm, its smooth stone flags interspersed with bushes and shrub, a sundial and fountains. Marble and stone used for the building were brought by Al-Jazzar from the Roman ruins of Ashkelon and Caesarea. Inside the high-domed mosque the walls are faced with marble slabs bordered by quotations from chapters of the Koran. Nearby are the tombs of Ahmed al-Jazzar, who built the mosque in 1781, and of his successor as Commander of Acre, Suleiman Pasha. To the west of the mosque is the bath-house of the Pasha. This picturesque building is now the municipal museum, housing a good collection of mediaeval ceramics, archaeological finds in the area and an artistic exhibition of local Moslem and Druze folklore.

Walking southwards towards the miniature harbour, where there are remnants of a Crusader jetty and light-house, you come upon three large Turkish caravanserais, or khans as they are called in Arabic. These are typical Eastern quadrangular inns with a large inner court, built as lodging places for caravan merchants and their animals.

The most ornate of the three khans is Khan el Umdan, Arabic for the Inn of Pillars, whose entrance is topped by a tall tower. Built in 1785, its wide courtyard is framed by pillars believed to have been brought from the Roman ruins of Caesarea. In the centre is a limestone fountain. The site of this khan was originally a Dominican monastery.

Across the adjoining small square, which fronts on the harbour, is the Khan el Afranj, Arabic for the Inn of the Franks, or Europeans. This, too, was built on the ruins of a Crusader site, believed to have been the convent whose nuns, during the final Moslem assault on the Crusader stronghold in 1291, deliberately disfigured themselves to avoid the attentions of Al-Ashraf Khalil's soldiers. In a corner of this khan is the Franciscan Monastery of St. Francis. St. Francis had visited Acre at the beginning of the 13th Century and it was here that the Franciscans established their first monastery in the East.

The third caravanserai is the Khan esh-Shawarda, with a square tower at its entrance. This is called Burj es-Sultan, and is a well preserved part of the original Crusader fortifications. Beyond the northern side of this khan is the old bazaar. On its northwestern side is the Sand Mosque, Jami er-Ramel in Arabic, built on the foundations of a Crusader church. A Crusader inscription on the mosque dating back to the 12th or 13th Century is an exhortation, in Latin, by "Master

Ebuli Fazie, builder of this chapel", to "men who pass along this street in charity I beg you pray for my soul."

Cutting back through the Shawarda inn and continuing eastwards, you come to the Turkish land-gate of the city, through which you now reach the new town.

Due north of the gate, in the northeastern corner of the old city wall, is a commanding Crusader tower, called the Accursed Tower no doubt because of the numerous assaults on this object of high strategic value during the battles in Crusader times.

Near the western sea wall, just north of the light-house, is the Greek Catholic St. Andrew's Church, built on the site of a Crusader church. In the next lane to the north is the Greek Orthodox St. George's Church, part of which is mediaeval. At the corner of the lane nearest the sea wall is a Bahai shrine. In an alley near the other end of the lane stands an old synagogue. This was the centre of the Jewish quarter in Turkish times.

Restoration work in Acre has been carried out by the Department for Landscaping and the Preservation of Historic Sites.

CARMEL AND HAIFA

The Carmel range, branching off to the northwest from the central Shomron mountains and ending at the Mediterranean, at the foot of Haifa's Mount Carmel, has an unusual place in the Biblical record. Unlike other noted sites mentioned in the Bible, it is not associated with any major military or political event. Indeed, ranged between the coastal plain and the Valley of Jezreel and reaching almost to the water's edge, it was a barrier to be by-passed both by trade caravans and the armies of warring empires. It is as a site of mysticism, a sanctuary, a place of retreat and a symbol of beauty that Carmel is remembered in the Biblical narrative, offering "one of the most sublime prospects of earth and sea and heaven", in the words of George Adam Smith. "Thine head upon thee is like Carmel. . . How fair and how pleasant art thou. . .", sings Solomon in the Song of Songs. (VII, 5). And Isaiah speaks of the "excellency of Carmel" (XXXV, 2).

From earliest times its heights held the altars of strange gods — among the wooded ridge and slopes are the remains of Canaanite shrines — and its caves offered solitude to hermits and hide-outs to fugitives. "Though they hide themselves in the top of Carmel," cried the prophet Amos, "I will search and take

The pre-historic caves of Mount Carmel.

them out thence. . ." (IX, 3) Small wonder that Carmel was the Biblical scene
of the great contest between monotheism and paganism when the prophet Elijah
challenged the prophets of Baal in the days of Ahab and Jezebel (I Kings XVIII).
The traditional site of this confrontation and of Elijah's miracle offering is El
Muhraka, some 17 miles by the mountain road southeast of Haifa, where there
now stands the Carmelite Monastery of St. Elijah. The spot where the false
prophets were put to death is believed to be the small mound in the valley below,
close to the banks of the Kishon river. ". . . and Elijah brought them down to the
brook Kishon, and slew them there." (Verse 40).

(This event, symbolic of the triumph of monotheism, makes Elijah a figure
revered also by Christians and Moslems. At the foot of the slopes near Haifa's
coastal suburb of Bat Galim is the sacred Jewish shrine, the "Cave of Elijah",
where the prophet is believed to have taken refuge on one of his frequent flights
from the anger of the king. It is a place holy also to Christians and Moslems).

Archaeological evidence shows that the Carmel range was inhabited as far back
as prehistoric times. A 1928–34 Anglo-American expedition made a remarkable
discovery in four large caves in a wadi that splits the seaward slopes just south
of Athlit. (These caves can be seen from the Tel Aviv-Haifa road). They found
human skeletons belonging to the intermediate type between Neanderthal man
and homo sapiens. Nearby were implements of bone and stone and jewellery
made of bone. It is believed that primitive man was drawn to this site by the
caves, which offered natural shelter, by the abundance of water and by the
sustenance provided by the wild life and fruit trees, notably the fig and carob.

Though there are few material remains of the intermittent and scattered settlement
on the Carmel during the Biblical period, there are relics of the Jewish resettlement
of the area after the destruction of the Second Temple. Synagogue remains were
found at Daliyat HaCarmel, now a Druze village, some three miles north of
Muhraka, and at the village of Isifia, two and a half miles further north. The
Isifia synagogue, belonging to the 5th Century A.D., had a partially preserved
floor mosaic depicting a seven-branched candelabrum, a ram's horn, plants
used in Jewish ritual, and a garland of flowers surrounding the Hebrew inscription
"Shalom el Yisrael" — "Peace be unto Israel".

During the Crusades, the Carmel heights, for the first time, were exploited for
strategic purposes. This was prompted by their proximity to the most important
ports in the country at that time, Acre, Athlit and Caesarea, through which the
Crusaders received their supplies and their reserves. To protect their rear, the
Crusaders made use of the Carmel range as part of their defensive network.
Remains of their fortifications are to be found at several places on the mountain-
side.

One of the religious legacies of the Crusaders is the Carmelite monastic Order,

founded here in the 13th Century with Elijah as patron saint. None of today's Carmelite buildings, however, dates from then, neither the monastery at Muhraka nor the more celebrated one in Haifa, close to the old lighthouse building, Stella Maris, on the French Carmel. (The Haifa monastery was used as a hospital by Napoleon's army during the siege of Acre in 1799). The only Carmelite remains from the Crusader period are the ruins of a chapel cut in the rock in the Valley of the Martyrs about a mile and a half due south of Stella Maris.

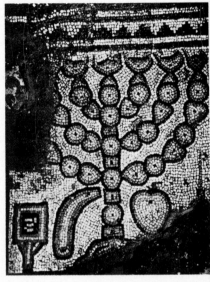

Menora, lulav, ethrog, shofar and incense burner depicted in 6th Century A.D. synagogue mosaic at Isifia.

The height which marks the northern extremity of the Carmel range is called Mount Carmel, its slopes and summit now covered by the charming residential suburbs of the town of Haifa, with the downtown dock area at its foot. Haifa today, with a population second only to that of Tel Aviv, is the main port city of the country and the centre of its heavy industry. Unlike Carmel, Haifa is nowhere mentioned in the Bible. The first reference to the place and its Jewish community occurs in the Talmudic literature of the 3rd Century A.D. It seems to have developed somewhat after the Moslem conquest, and when the Crusaders first reached it in 1100 A.D., Haifa's Jewish and Arab communities are reported to have joined in battle against the common enemy. With the rise of Acre as the main port under the Crusaders, whatever modest importance Haifa had enjoyed now declined. Nor was it regained with the Crusader departure at the end of the 13th Century.

The Haifa of those days was smaller than the smallest of today's suburbs — it was possibly no more than a fishing village — and it was confined to the foot of the mount, probably at the tip of the peninsula where the suburb of Bat Galim now stands. About a mile to the south of this spot is the site of ancient Shikmona, twin village, in those days, to Haifa. A fine old mosaic of uncertain date (probably 5th Century A.D.) was found among its ruins some years ago and is now on exhibition in Haifa's museum of antiquities.

ATHLIT

Nine miles south of Haifa, the smooth, sand-edged Mediterranean coast curves into a sickle-shaped bay and then suddenly erupts into a curious promontory. It curves again on the other side, forming a second bay. The rock and its two flanking inlets, which gave sheltered anchorage to small vessels, was the location of a modest seafaring settlement established by the Phoenicians in days of old. Many centuries later, the Crusaders selected this promontory, known as Athlit, as the site on which to build one of their largest castles in the country. So formidable was this stronghold that even the few ruins which have remained to this day bear powerful witness to Crusader skill and might. Athlit can now be reached by a two mile access road from the main Haifa–Tel Aviv coastal highway.

The castle was erected by the Crusader Order of Templars in the year 1218. The Christians had lost Jerusalem some thirty years earlier, and the centre of their administrative power had shifted from the Holy City to Acre in the north. They then began to fortify the strategic locations in the limited areas still left to them — western and central Galilee and the northern part of the coast. Athlit was marked as a good site for such a stronghold. It commanded the coastal pass, made narrow in this area by the encroachment of Mount Carmel whose western slopes reach to within a few miles of the water's edge. The promontory, a peninsula in miniature, offered natural defence on its three seaward sides to Crusaders who were masters of the sea. And the harbours which had served the Phoenicians could now be used to disembark pilgrims — as well as emergency troops rushed by ship if the knights at Athlit were hard-pressed. A fourth, unexpressed, virtue was the ease offered by this site of a quick get-away. Advantage was to be taken of this very quality when the end came.

In the building of their castle the Templars were aided by energetic pilgrims. As a tribute to them, it was named Castrum Peregrinorum in Latin and Chastel Pelerin in old French — Castle of Pilgrims. In time, it became a pilgrims' castle in another sense; for up until the Crusader collapse in 1291, Athlit was the chief port of entry for Christian pilgrims. It was convenient; there was room on the rock to serve as a transit area; and the Templars were happy to take away business from the merchants of Acre whom they despised.

Unlike most other great castles, Athlit was never taken by siege. It was attacked several times during the seventy-three years of its existence, but it held out. And it was still intact when, in May 1291, Acre fell, climaxing a series of disasters which put an end to the Crusader kingdom. With no further military purpose to be served, the last Christian stronghold in Palestine was evacuated. This took place in August of the same year, the knights of Athlit walking the few steps from the castle to their waiting ships which carried them off to Cyprus. Their departure marked the final fall of the curtain for the Crusades.

But this was not known at the time. Fearing a possible fresh invasion from Europe, the Moslems destroyed all the Crusader ports along the Palestine coast. The piers and jetties were smashed and the harbours sealed with stones from the walls. The records of later travellers reveal that though a good part of the fortifications of Athlit must have been demolished at that time, many of the inner buildings were relatively untouched, and these seem to have withstood the

The Crusader "Castle of Pilgrims" at Athlit.

batterings of tide and wind for more than five hundred years. They were then laid low by the earthquake of 1837. And ten years later, Ibrahim Pasha carried off ship-loads of their masonry to rebuild Acre. His example was followed by others over the years. Yet despite the depredations of nature and man, what is left today of the Pilgrims' Castle is impressive.

The structural plan of this stronghold was determined by the shape and location of the promontory on which it stood. This is a rough, jagged rectangle of rock, averaging 850 feet in length and 480 feet in width. It looks, in aerial view, like the profile of a crouching lion, with shoulders, mane and fore-paws jutting out into the water. Northern, western and southern sides of this rock were thus protected by the sea. Only its landward side was in need of basic fortification. Accordingly, on the seaward sides, the Templars built only a single wall, massive enough and strengthened by several towers, but nothing else of a defensive nature. A section of the northern side of this wall remains today, together with the ruins of two towers. The area enclosed by the wall served as a transit compound for pilgrims. (In the final years of the British Mandate, shortly before the establishment of independent Israel, the compound was used for a different kind of "pilgrim" — the "illegal" Jewish immigrants, survivors of Nazism, who were caught trying to reach the Promised Land by crashing through the British ban on their entry). Preparing the main defence works on the eastern, or landward, side, the Templars first cut a moat, 80 feet wide and 20 feet deep, right across the neck of the promontory, from north to south, thus isolating it from the adjoining land mass. In time of emergency, this moat could be flooded by the sea from either end, turning the promontory into an island. This was the first obstacle which an attacking force would encounter. To the immediate west, covering the moat and its approaches, was an outer wall, 50 feet high and 20 feet thick, strengthened by three rectangular towers rising to a height of 90 feet. Entry to and exit from the towers were by postern gate, each equipped with portcullis. Behind this wall the Crusaders constructed their huge inner wall with two enormous rectangular towers. The wall of one of these towers still stands to a height of 110 feet, dominating the castle ruins. Many of its stones, dressed and well bossed, some of them 4 feet long and 2 feet deep, were taken from ancient masonry found by the Crusaders on the site.

In an assault on the fortress, the Crusaders could command considerable defensive power from troops manning the two walls and their total of five bastions. The first wall and towers were lower than the defensive works to their rear, so as not to obstruct the latter's field of fire. And the two great rear towers were in line with the centre of the intervals between the three front towers, affording complementary angles of fire. Thus, no part of the approach area was unprotected.

Behind these triple defence lines — moat, outer and inner walls — the Templars constructed their castle buildings. Most of these have disappeared, but from excavations and some clearance work carried out by the Mandatory Government's Department of Antiquities in 1930, they seem to have been handsome structures. The storage chambers near the big towers and along part of the southern wall are in a good state of preservation. And the large hall with vaulted roof near the western edge of the rock is an excellent example of Crusader architecture. The most important ruin on the site is part of a hexagonal chapel near the centre of the promontory, close to the south wall and to one of the original landing stages of the harbour. From the 18th Century English traveller Bishop Pococke we know that this was one of three absidal chapels attached to a large round church, modelled after the Templar headquarters' circular shrine in the Dome of the Rock in Jerusalem, which the Moslems had erected within the Temple of Solomon compound. The Order of Templars built similar churches, exact copies of their Chapter-church, in several European cities. When the English Bishop visited Athlit, church and chapels, though ruined, were still standing; and so he could describe the main structure as a "fine lofty church of ten sides, built in slightly Gothic taste". Such records of travellers, together with the ruins on the site, enable us to conjure up the 13th Century buildings which made the Castle of Pilgrims a Crusader pride.

Marble statue of fertility goddess found during excavation of Roman theatre in Caesarea.

CAESAREA

Caesarea, midway along the Mediterranean coast between Tel Aviv and Haifa, is an archaeologist's dream and a sportsman's paradise. You can loll in the sand beneath the arch of an early Roman aqueduct; leap into the sparkling water from a pier which rests upon Roman and Crusader boulders; drive a golf ball through nineteen hundred years from a 20th Century course into a 1st Century hippodrome; and, in the early autumn, listen to the world's virtuosi making music in the original Roman theatre under the eastern skies. Caesarea is indeed a happy conjunction of history and beauty. Recent excavations have uncovered the remains of buildings belonging to the Roman, Byzantine and Crusader periods.

The site on which Caesarea was to rise made a modest entry into history in the middle of the 3rd Century B.C. as a small anchorage, built by the Phoenicians when they captured the Sharon strip of the Palestine coast and established a chain of minor naval colonies. They called it Strato's Tower. It was mentioned by the merchant Zenon a century later as a place where he distributed rations on behalf of Apollonius, treasurer of Egypt. At the end of the 2nd Century B.C. it was incorporated into the Hasmonean kingdom by Alexander Jannai. But the conquest of Jerusalem by the Roman general Pompey in 63 B.C. brought new masters to Strato's Tower. Judea was pruned of its coastal towns and these were placed under the rule of the Roman governor of Syria. It was still a place of limited importance.

It rose to greatness under Herod. When Caesar Augustus confirmed him as king of Judea and extended his domain to the coastal region, Herod showed his gratitude by building a lasting monument to his royal Roman patron. On the site of Strato's Tower, he started construction of a town and port in the year 22 B.C. Twelve years later he was able to inaugurate one of the most striking port-cities of the period, naming it in honour of the Roman emperor. His choice of site is well explained by the ancient historian Josephus Flavius: "When he observed that there was a city by the sea-side that was much decayed, but that the place, by the happiness of its situation, was capable of great improvements, he rebuilt it all with white stone, and adorned it with several most splendid palaces ... for the case was this, that all the sea-shore between Dora and Joppa, in the middle between which this city is situated, had no good haven, insomuch that every one that sailed from Phoenicia for Egypt was obliged to lie in the stormy sea ... But the king overcame nature, and built a haven larger than was the Peiraeion (near Athens) ... (with a) quay which ran round the entire haven."

The deep-sea harbour, "limen Sebasti" — Augustus' port — complete with quay and breakwater, was a daring engineering feat. It rapidly turned Caesarea Sebastos, Caesarea Palaestina, or Caesarea Maritima, as it was variously called, into one of the leading maritime cities in the eastern Mediterranean.

The town itself was, by ancient standards, of majestic size and grandeur. This we know both from the relics and from the eye-witness report of Josephus, who visited the town when it was just about fifty years old and was vastly impressed: "... abutting the harbour were houses, also of white stone, and upon it converged the streets of the town, laid at equal distances apart. On the eminence facing the harbour-mouth stood Caesar's temple, remarkable for its beauty and grand proportions ... He also built other edifices, the amphitheatre, theatre, and market place, all constructed in a style worthy of the name which the city bore. He further appointed games every fifth year, and called

A synagogue capital decorated with a menora, found in the Jewish quarter of 5th Century Caesarea.

Articles from the treasure of gold, 11th–12th Century A.D., found during excavations of Roman port warehouses in Caesarea.

them in like manner Caesar's Games." Outside the city walls, Herod built a hippodrome.

Such was its splendour that in the year 6 A.D., ten years after Herod's death, it became the seat of the Roman procurators of Judea. From then on, except for a three-year interlude when it was once again part of the kingdom of Judea under Herod Agrippa I, Caesarea came under direct Roman rule.

It was the Jews of Caesarea who, in the year 66 A.D., raised the standard of revolt against the Romans, whose general, Vespasian, was headquartered in the town. Riots broke out between the Jews and Caesarea's large Syrian community, and the Romans sided with the Syrians. The Jews fought them both, and in the process lost 20,000, who were massacred. This touched off the Great Jewish War which ended four years later in the fall of Jerusalem and the destruction of the Second Temple. Titus, after sacking Jerusalem, came to Caesarea, carrying with him the spoils of the Temple and thousands of prisoners, to celebrate his victory. This was marked on 4 October in the year 70 A.D. with a formidable spectacle of "games" in the amphitheatre, in which 2,500 Jewish prisoners perished.

Caesarea blossomed in the 2nd and 3rd Centuries. The Jews returned, built synagogues and schools and prominent scholars taught the Law of Moses. The city also figured in the development of early Christianity. It was here that Peter had baptised the centurion Cornelius; here that Paul was imprisoned and held the conversations with Agrippa recorded in Chapter 26 of Acts; and from here he set sail for Rome. In the 3rd Century, the celebrated scholar Origenes established the famous school of Caesarea, a centre of Christian learning renowned for the accuracy of its copies of the Septuagint. The tradition was continued by his pupil Eusebius, author of "Onomastikon" and bishop of the town at the beginning of the 4th Century. When the newly converted Constantine founded the capital of Constantinople, he endowed its churches with 50 copies of the Bible, written on vellum in Caesarea. The famous Codex Sinaiticus, now in the British Museum, is believed by scholars to be one of these copies.

After the Arab conquest in 639 A.D., Caesarea remained opulent for a time — travellers described it as "heaven on earth" — but Herod's splendid harbour fell into decay and the town declined in importance. In 1101, it fell to the Crusaders in a combined assault by king Baldwin I and the Genoese fleet. When Benjamin of Tudela visited it in 1170, he found "about 200 Jews" there. In 1187, it was recaptured by the Saracens under Saladin, after his decisive victory at the Horns of Hattin. In the next 40 years, as the scene of ding-dong battle, it changed hands five times, returning to Christian domination in 1228. But it was not until 1251, when the Crusader exploits in the Holy Land were approaching their end, that Louis IX of France built the "impregnable" fortifications of Caesarea, whose

The Crusader moat in Caesarea, built by Louis IX in middle of 13th Century A.D.

remains may be seen today. The last battle took place in 1265, when the sultan Baibars showed that the Crusader defences were "pregnable" after all by capturing the city. From then on, it faded from the map, abandoned by man, buried by sand dunes.

Archaeological excavations have been conducted by the Missione Archaeologica Italiana a Caesarea Instituto Lombardo, of Milan, under the direction of Professor Antonio Frova, who unearthed the Roman theatre in 1961; by the American industrialist and engineer, Edwin Link, using his own specially constructed vessel for submarine study, who carried out a remarkable under-water exploration of Herod's submerged harbour in 1960; by Professor Michael Avi-Yonah, of the Hebrew University, who excavated the area north of the harbour in 1956 and again in 1962; and by Dr. Avraham Negev, of the Hebrew University, on behalf of the Department for Landscaping and the Preservation of Historic Sites, who excavated the Crusader city and directed the clearance and restoration work in the area. Excavations continue.

Caesarea is reached by a short turn-off road three miles north of Hadera on the Tel Aviv-Haifa highway. The first site of antiquity, seen through a stone gate decorated with a cross just beyond the entrance to the golf course, is the Roman hippodrome. This has not yet been excavated, and it is much overgrown, but it is worth a quick inspection to gain an idea of the scale of Herodian architecture. This race course could hold 20,000 spectators. In the centre is an obelisk. Near it are three granite pillars. These are old Roman "horse-frighteners". Polished smooth and turned to the sun, they would reflect a blinding beam in the eyes of the horses, scaring them, so the stewards hoped, into speed.

Almost opposite the hippodrome is a newly built side road, running north, which forks in front of a low mound. At the top of this mound is a fine 5th-6th Century mosaic, the original floor of a Byzantine church, with beautifully executed presentations of birds and animals. It was discovered in 1957.

The left fork continues to the early Roman aqueduct on the sea-shore. Up to a short time ago, only a single arch was visible. The others were all buried under dunes. When the sand was cleared, an immense stretch of the original aqueduct stood revealed, its arches and conduit well preserved. This solidly built structure brought sweet water to Caesarea from the mountain springs in the north.

Close by are the remains of 4th-7th Century synagogues discovered by the Hebrew University expedition of 1956 under the direction of Professor Avi-Yonah. Among the ruins were found fragments of mosaics and decorated marble capitals adorned with the menora, the seven-branched candelabrum. Resuming excava-

Roman columns of granite used to buttress Crusader port tower at Caesarea. ▶

Recently excavated Roman aqueduct at Caesarea.

tions of this promising site in 1962, Avi-Yonah laid bare other relics of importance, including a 4th Century synagogue within whose compound he found a magnificent hoard of 3,700 bronze coins. The latest of these was struck by Gallus Caesar, whose reign began in the year 351 A.D. In the stratum above were the remains of a 5th Century synagogue. Close by were the ruins of a large Byzantine dwelling house. It was near this site, north of the mole, that Avraham Negev brought to light remains identifying the spot as the original location of Strato's Tower.

Returning to the Caesarea road, just beyond the hippodrome are Byzantine ruins dating to the 5th-6th Centuries. Their proudest features are however two earlier objects — the impressive statues at the foot of the broad staircase. Both are Roman. The one of white marble is 2nd Century; the other, of red porphyry, is 3rd Century. The statues were brought here to enrich the structure which, in the words of the Greek inscription in the mosaic floor, "the mayor Flavius Stategius built out of public funds . . . in a good hour."

A few hundred yards beyond, the road reaches the eastern gate of the Crusader city, which was the main gate. From here one receives the best general view of the ancient remains uncovered by the extensive new archaeological excavations. Lapped by the sea is the recently repaired mole of the Crusader harbour, rebuilt on the site of the Byzantine and the original Roman port. Inland is the Crusader city proper, which was enclosed by a wall on its three landward sides and covered an area of 35 acres. (The Roman city was about six times as large). The wall was protected by a moat, 30 feet wide, which has been cleared and is intact. The sloping embankment, an additional fortification of the wall, is also in good condition. It rises from 30 to 45 feet above the base of the moat.

Each period of settlement used the remains of earlier structures as a source of building materials. Statues taken from Roman temples were used by the Byzantines. Floors of early Arab houses were made of marble facings torn down from Roman walls. Lintels, friezes and columns, specially brought from Italy and Greece hundreds of years earlier, were used by the Crusaders to strengthen their fortifications. Massive pillars of porphyry were hewn into slabs for use as millstones. Caesarea, thanks largely to Herod, was a seemingly inexhaustible source of building supplies not only for later settlements on the same site but also, within the last 200 years, for Acre, Jaffa — and even distant Venice.

The main gate was reached by a bridge supported by four pointed arches. The preservation of the four original piers and the springers of the arches made it possible to reconstruct the bridge. Close by are the 30 feet high remains of the original tower which protected the bridge.

In this very area, the excavators discovered the remains of an earlier Crusader

Unique inscription of the name of Pontius Pilate, recently discovered in Caesarea.

gate, of the direct approach type, built before the construction of the moat when the city was fortified only by a wall. Louis IX built the moat, strengthened the wall with an embankment, and added a large oblong passage-way at rightangles to the old gate with an opening at its northern end, thereby converting it into an indirect approach gate. It was found in good condition, with only the roof and upper storey missing. Most of the arches and pilasters, complete with elaborate capitals, were found in situ, and what was missing was discovered in the debris. This made it possible to effect a faithful reconstruction of the gate. Also found on the site were grooves for the portcullis and sockets for the hinges of the iron doors.

Inside the city, hard by this main gate is a Crusader street, paved with large blocks of marble taken from Roman buildings. It runs westward, and linked the gate with the harbour. To the immediate south of this street were the first, hurriedly-built, Crusader fortifications, constructed of whatever materials there were to hand — large Corinthian capitals, Attic bases, and fragments of friezes and columns.

To the north, the ground rises abruptly. Trial digs showed it to be an artificial rise, covering the foundations of a huge building on one side and five large vaulted constructions on the other, all Herodian. The building may well have been the temple Herod built "on the eminence facing the harbour-mouth" of which Josephus wrote. The vaulted constructions, one of which was intact and contained numerous Byzantine storage jars, were built by the Romans probably as port warehouses, and they continued to be so used by the Byzantines.

The summit of this rise is now occupied by the remains of two Crusader buildings. One is a cathedral which was never completed. The three apses at its eastern end are of excellent workmanship. Beneath the nave, and serving as its support, is the Roman vaulted warehouse which is intact. The northern aisle rests upon one of the vaulted halls which had collapsed. The second Crusader building, preserved only in its foundations and part of the upper structure, was built round a large court. Eight Corinthian capitals bearing engravings of the cross were found in the debris.

While levelling a path outside the mediaeval city just south of the moat, the excavators discovered a complex of Byzantine buildings, many of them with mosaic paving.

The fine Roman theatre excavated by the Italian expedition is located about 300 yards south of the harbour. During their dig, the archaeologists made the historic discovery of a stone inscribed with the name of Pontius Pilate, Roman procurator of Judea at the time of the Crucifixion. This is unique. Up to now, the name of Pontius Pilate was known only from the Gospels and the writings of Josephus.

Part of the theatre site is still covered by a profusion of broken marble columns and finely fashioned capitals. But the semi-circular, multi-tiered auditorium and the well of the stage, scooped out of the cliff above the blue waters of the sea, have now been cleared. They present a sight of beauty. The rulers of those times were neither the most humane nor the most refined people in history. But they knew how to build. And they knew where. The theatre is a monument to their skill and taste.

TEL AVIV—JAFFA

In a land replete with sites of antiquity, Tel Aviv prided itself on its newness, and with some reason. It was founded as recently as 1909 by a group of visionary Jewish residents of Jaffa on the sand dunes to the immediate north of that ancient Mediterranean port. From a cluster of houses erected on the dunes it has grown into the largest city in Israel, the busy centre of commerce, banking, light industry, publishing, music, theatre and the arts, and Jaffa is now its appendage. The dunes have disappeared beneath the green lawns, boulevards, modern hotels and apartment houses of a Twentieth Century city, with only the ribbon of sandy beach to recall the nature of its original foundations.

But nowhere in Israel can any settlement emerge and develop without meeting the remains of ancient habitation. And as fast expanding Tel Aviv has burst its way eastwards and northwards, the builder's pick has inevitably struck some relic of antiquity. The founding fathers little guessed that not far from the spot on which they were building what they thought was the first Jewish city, archaeologists would find remains of Jewish settlements which flourished in the time of David and Solomon and the kings of Israel who followed, were revived by the Jews who returned from Babylon, and were continued intermittently through the Hasmonean, Herodian and late Roman periods.

The first scholar to undertake a dig to determine the history of Tel Aviv's environs was the late E. L. Sukenik, Professor of Archaeology at the Hebrew University. In 1927 he started a series of excavations at Tell el Jerisha, an artificial mound on the south bank of the river Yarkon, about two miles due east of today's Tel Aviv port, and he found levels of settlement going back to the beginning of the Hyksos period in the 18th Century B.C. Until then, the mound had been associated only with the 18th Century A.D., for Napoleon, who captured nearby

Jaffa in 1799, used it as a riverside rest encampment for his troops, and it had accordingly been known as Napoleon's Hill. (Contrary to the widely accepted view, it was not used as a gun position during Napoleon's attack on Jaffa. His guns were sited further south, closer to their target.)

The fortified Hyksos settlement was surrounded by a wall ten feet thick, built of sun-dried mud bricks, its lower part strengthened by an ingenious embankment comprising layers of bricks, crushed sandstone and beaten earth. Among the ruins of buildings within the city compound were found vessels of high quality, infant burials in pottery jars, and a kiln for firing ceramics. (In 1950, Dr. Yaacov Kaplan unearthed a cemetery typical of the period, with 18 scattered burial pits and niches cut in their walls to receive the bodies. The mouth of the niche was sealed by stones and clay. Buried, too, were pottery vessels — bowls, plates, jars and perfume flasks — and the personal effects of the deceased, battle axe and sword for the men, jewellery for the women.) The site on the hill also yielded to Dr. Sukenik's spade relics of later settlements belonging to the Canaanite, Philistine and king David periods.

Ten years after he started digging at Tell el Jerisha, Sukenik, together with the archaeologist S. Yeivin, followed it up with a dig at Tell Kedadi, on the estuary of the Yarkon, only a few hundred yards north of the new Sheraton and Hilton hotels. Their most notable finds were remains of the keep of a fort built during the time of king Solomon, and ruins belonging to the Roman period.

These pioneer researches in the area were given fresh impetus after the establishment of the State of Israel in 1948, and since then no less than twenty archaeological sites have been excavated in the populous belt stretching from Jaffa to a few hundred yards north of the river Yarkon. Relics of ancient settlement are to be found today in the very heart of the city, just off main streets, new housing suburbs and modern office buildings. The digs were carried out by Professor Benjamin Mazar and by the archaeologist who has made a special study of this town, Dr. Yaacov Kaplan. Kaplan, indeed, has directed excavations on seventeen of the sites. Their researches have contributed much to our knowledge both of this area and of the history of the country.

We now know that about a mile east of the Sheraton hotel, at a site called Givat Rehov Habashan, there was a New Stone Age (Neolithic) settlement dating to the 5th millennium B.C. In this mound and in another one nearby, at the top of one of the main roads of the city, Rehov Jabotinsky, Chalcolithic remains were discovered, belonging to the intermediate period between the Stone and Bronze Ages. The most interesting of these finds were the typical two-handle pottery churn, beautifully fashioned, of the type found some years later in Beersheba; and a characteristic feature of the culture of the period, the ossuaries used in secondary burials. These ossuaries were shaped like miniature dwelling houses,

and this enabled the people to bury the bones of their dead outside their settlement, while retaining, in symbolic form, the earlier custom of burial in the home. Fine specimens of similar ossuaries of the period were also found at Azur, a few miles southeast of Tel Aviv on the Jerusalem road. Between the Rehov Habashan site and the beach, at a spot called Givat Beth Hamitbachayim, Kaplan discovered a subterranean Chalcolithic settlement, similar to those found in Beersheba by the French archaeologist Jean Perrot.

The most extensive excavations of a single site in Tel Aviv undertaken after 1948 were those directed by Professor Mazar at Tell Kasile. It is located on the north bank of the Yarkon, close to the main bridge which carries the coastal highway out of the city towards Haifa. The first settlement on this site was found to have been established by the invading "Sea Peoples", among them the Philistines, in the 12th Century B.C. Mazar uncovered remains of brick built structures, one containing two smelting furnaces strewn with copper slag. A later Philistine stratum bore the ruins of houses, some with stone-paved courtyards, workshops, and storage chambers with numerous large vessels for storing wine and oil. This city was clearly a trading centre, maintaining commercial relations with Phoenician ports on the Mediterranean coast and the islands, exporting to them oil, wine, corn and copper artefacts.

The excavations showed that this settlement had been destroyed in the 10th Century B.C., probably by king David, and an Israelite city built on its ruins, with the typical four-chambered house of the Davidic period. In the time of Solomon, there were architectural changes, with the introduction of stone-based brick pillars to support the roof. Oil and wine presses, silos, ovens and millstones may be seen today. Also found were two important 8th Century B.C. ostraca — inscribed potsherds — written in early Hebrew script. One may be described as a despatch slip, recording the export of a quantity of olive oil from the royal storehouses of this Israeli city to a Mediterranean port. It was signed by the local controller of exports. The other was a note of the import of 30 shekels of fine gold. This settlement lasted until the year 732 when it was destroyed with the conquest of the country by Tiglath Pileser III.

From the relics and the inscribed potsherds, it was evident that this city, too, throughout the period of the Israel kings, was a centre of trade with Phoenicia. This led Mazar to suggest that it was here, and not Jaffa, to which the cedars of Lebanon were shipped and from here sent overland to Jerusalem in the 10th Century B.C. for the building of Solomon's Temple. And since the excavations also showed that the city was rebuilt during the Persian period by the Jews who returned from Babylonian exile, and developed into the administrative centre of the Yarkon river region, he thinks that the same route was followed in the 6th Century B.C. for the cedars shipped to Zerubbabel for the building of the

Ostracon — inscribed potsherd — in early Hebrew script from the Royal storehouse of Israelite city of Tell Kasile, 8th Century B.C.

The Tell Kasile excavations.

Second Temple. Both Biblical quotations which report the events — II Chronicles II, 16 and Ezra III, 7 — record, in the original Hebrew, that the cedars were sent from Lebanon to the "sea of Joppa". (The English translation of the Chronicles quotation is "to Joppa", but its accuracy is questioned). It is Mazar's theory that in the days of David and Solomon, Jaffa was just outside their borders and under foreign hegemony, so they would have been unable to use this port. Instead, they used one near to it, a couple of miles away but close enough to be designated within the "sea of Joppa". This alternative port, thinks Mazar, was Tell Kasile, conveniently situated on the bank of the river Yarkon and close to its estuary. In those days, the mouth of the river had not yet silted up, and Tell Kasile must have offered a quiet, sheltered, inland anchorage, protected from storms and pirates, where vessels could turn in from the open sea to load and unload and take on water.

Of Tell Kasile's Hellenistic, Roman and Byzantine remains, the most impressive are the buildings belonging to the Herodian part of the Roman era. Thereafter come ruins of the poor and primitive buildings of the early Arab period, and only the characteristic glazed potsherds of the 13th to 15th Century A.D. period of the Mamelukes.

The excavation of the Tell Kasile cemetery was undertaken later by Dr. Kaplan.

Incidentally, close to these excavations is the new Haaretz Museum which contains one of the finest collections in the world of ancient glass, left to Tel-Aviv by the late Dr. Walter Moses. It consists of an almost complete range of glass vessels and artefacts found in the country from the Bronze Age to the Byzantines.

The ancient names of the archaeological sites in Tel Aviv proper are not known. Names like Tell Jerishe and Tell Kasile are fairly new. By contrast, Jaffa, the southern section of today's city, is a name very well known in the world of antiquity by any one of its variants — Yafo, Yofi, Yafa, Joppa, Jaffa, and today, in Hebrew, once again Yafo. The meaning of its Hebrew origin is "beautiful", and it has about it the beauty natural to all hill cities overlooking the sea — for the ancient site of Jaffa is the hill above the harbour. But no city of antiquity can be without its legends, and so some hold that it was named after Noah's son Japhet and that it was founded by him after the deluge. Jaffa also has its place in Greek mythology as the location of the Andromeda legend. It was on a rock rising from the sea just below the hill that the beautiful princess Andromeda was said to have been chained as a sacrifice to appease the sea monster. But along came Perseus with his winged shoes, slew the monster and unshackled the fair maiden. As late as Roman times the inhabitants of Jaffa are said to have done a roaring trade exhibiting bits of the monster's bones and of Andromeda's chains to credulous visitors. To this day, one of the crags near the entrance to Jaffa harbour is known as Andromeda's Rock.

Also unlike the sites excavated in Tel Aviv, Jaffa has a *recorded* history of three thousand five hundred years. It was already a sufficiently well established settlement to have found mention in the 15th Century B.C. records of the Egyptian pharaoh Thutmose III. And it also appears in the 14th Century B.C. Tell el-Amarna letters. The first Biblical reference to this city appears in the Book of Joshua (xix, 46) where it is listed as one of the places falling within the area assigned to the tribe of Dan. In the Second Book of Chronicles (ii, 16) Jaffa is mentioned in the description by the king of Tyre to the king of Israel of the method of sending him cedars for the Temple: "And we will cut wood out of Lebanon, as much as thou shalt need: and we will bring it to thee in flotes by sea to Joppa; and thou shalt carry it up to Jerusalem." The Book of Ezra (iii, 7) records that the same route was to be followed for the cargoes of cedars sent for the construction of the Second Temple: "They gave . . . meat, and drink, and oil, unto them of Zidon, and to them of Tyre, to bring cedar trees from Lebanon to the sea of Joppa. . .".*

The most widely known mention of Jaffa in the Bible appears in the tale of the reluctant prophet Jonah. It was from here that he took ship to evade his divine mission and ended up in the belly of a whale: "Now the word of the Lord came unto Jonah the son of Amitai, saying, Arise, go to Nineveh, that great city, and cry against it; for their wickedness is come up before me. But Jonah rose up to flee unto Tarshish from the presence of the Lord, and went down to Joppa; and he found a ship going to Tarshish. . ." (Jonah i, 1–3).

Jaffa is recorded as among the cities conquered by Sennacherib in 701 B.C. when the Assyrian forces swept down the coast from the north driving all before them. It knew little peace during the next four hundred years, though the pattern of its life remained relatively unchanged until its conquest by Alexander the Great in 332 B.C., who turned it into a Greek city. During the nationwide Jewish revolt under the Hasmoneans against the authority of Antioch, in the 2nd Century B.C., the Hellenised population of Jaffa dealt harshly with its community of Jews, forcing them aboard vessels and drowning them at sea. They had counted on a Hasmonean defeat. But the revolt succeeded. And Jonathan, brother of Judah the Maccabee, conquered Jaffa in 148 B.C., a conquest consolidated by another brother, Simon, who fortified and developed Jaffa into a Jewish port city and suppressed all forms of Greek paganism.

Even under Rome Jaffa retained its thoroughly Jewish character, its community

---

* For a different interpretation of these verses and the suggestion that the cedars were brought not to Jaffa but to the nearby port of Tell Kasile within the "sea" of Jaffa, see previous page.

rigidly adhering to the Mosaic law and maintaining strong links with the Patriots of Jerusalem. When the great Jewish rebellion started, the Jews of Jaffa were among the stoutest fighters, but the town fell before the Roman Legions in 68 A.D. Several decades later, Jews began to return to Jaffa. From then until the 4th Century, it achieved renown as a centre of Jewish learning where outstanding Talmudic sages dwelt and taught.

Jaffa was conquered by the Moslems in 636. Almost half a millennium later, it became the scene of hard fought battles with the Crusaders. The Christians held it for most of the time they were in the country, prizing it as the port closest to Jerusalem and the most convenient debarkation point for their overseas reserves. They lost it to Saladin in 1196, but Richard the Lion Heart retook it a few years later. The Crusaders lost it again shortly afterwards and again recaptured it in 1204. They then put up strong fortifications, surrounding the city with a wall strengthened by twenty-four towers and a citadel built on top of the hill. But when the final onslaught came by the sultan Baibars in 1268, their fortifications were of no help. The victorious Baibars ordered them destroyed.

Jaffa revived, however, in the 14th Century and became once again a seafaring city. It was still enjoying a modest prosperity when Napoleon captured it in 1799 on his way northward to Acre; but he abandoned it a few months later when he abandoned his siege of Acre. At that time, there was a significant community of Jewish immigrants who had arrived earlier in the century. They were considerably reinforced by the first Zionist pioneers of the 19th Century who entered the Promised Land through Jaffa harbour and used the city as a base while organising their new life. They established the first Zionist settlements only a few miles south of the port. And, as we have seen, it was a group of Jews from Jaffa who moved off in 1909 to found, on its northern dunes, the new city of Tel Aviv. The bitter street fighting in the Arab-Jewish war of 1948 ravaged the border areas between the two adjoining cities, leaving a rubble-strewn waste which has now been cleared but not yet built up. After the establishment of Israel, the two cities became one, officially named Tel Aviv-Jaffa.

None of Jaffa's recorded history had found tangible expression in ruins and relics before 1948, when the first archaeological dig was carried out on the high ground above the harbour by the late P. L. O. Guy. But neither that nor the dig that followed in 1952 was successful in uncovering the earliest periods of settlement. Only with the excavations by Kaplan in 1955–1961 was the ancient history of this city brought to light.

Jaffa's first mention in pre-Biblical documents was in the 15th Century B.C. But Kaplan found remains dating back to the 18th Century B.C., similar to those found by Professor Sukenik at Tell Jerishe. These were parts of the 20 foot thick

wall of a Hyksos citadel, also buttressed by an embankment of bricks, crushed sandstone and beaten earth.

A remarkable find in a later stratum made it possible to give it an exact and absolute date — the hope of every archaeologist when he begins a dig. This was the city gate upon whose stone posts was inscribed the name of the pharaoh Rameses II, discovered in one of the levels of settlement when Jaffa was under Egyptian tutelage. Since the dates of this pharaoh are known — 1301 to 1234 B.C. — the inscription offered an accurate dating both of the level in which it was found and of those which came immediately before and after. Incidentally, the Exodus of the Children of Israel from Egypt is believed by some scholars to have taken place during the reign of this very pharaoh, Rameses II.

Also found were the ruins of the last Canaanite city on the site, whose gates showed signs of having been burnt in the 12th Century B.C.; remains of the city rebuilt by the Jews in the time of Ezra and Nehemiah; parts of a thick wall belonging to the 3rd Century B.C.; a statue of Aphrodite and three inscribed potsherds in Greek, from the 2nd Century B.C.; ruins of a wall constructed during the period of Hasmonean rule and a hoard of bronze coins struck by the grand-nephew of Judah the Macabee, Alexander Jannai (103–76 B.C.); and remains from the Roman period. Most of these ruins may be seen today on the site of the excavations.

The ancient cemetery of the Jews of Jaffa who gathered in that city after the Bar Kochba revolt was discovered by the French archaeologist Clermont Ganneau at the end of the last century. It is situated about a mile to the east of the excavations, part of it within the compound now occupied by the Russian church and monastery near Abu Kebir. In 1871, Clermont Ganneau found some marble tombstones bearing inscriptions in Hebrew, Aramaic and Greek, their dates covering the years between the 2nd and 4th Centuries A.D. Many of these slabs are now in European museums.

Of the centuries that followed, little remains in Jaffa beyond the sites and the legends and the old world charm of its narrow alleyways and cobbled passages that dart mysteriously through the Turkish buildings and walls. However, across the road from the excavations, on the slope overlooking the harbour, is the Franciscan Monastery of St. Peter, built in the last century but standing on the foundations of a mediaeval fort. This was the 13th Century Crusader citadel. Steps from the monastery courtyard lead down to two well-preserved chambers of this citadel, one of them circular in shape, with a shallow-domed ceiling, and firing embrasures cut in its walls. The monastery commemorates the visit of Peter the Apostle to Jaffa, whither he was summoned to awaken from death "a certain disciple named Tabitha", and where he "tarried many days . . . with one Simon a tanner". (Acts ix, 36, 43). The traditional site of the house where he

stayed is in a winding alley lower down the slope where a 1730 mosque now stands: "And now send men to Joppa, and call for one Simon, whose surname is Peter: He lodgeth with one Simon a tanner, whose house is by the sea side ..." This old mosque is indeed close to the sea, hard by the lighthouse. The legendary Tomb of Tabitha, subject of Peter's miracle, is said to be a burial cave in the courtyard of the Russian monastery at Abu Kebir which covers the site of the ancient Jewish cemetery.

The hill of the excavations is reached by a side road that runs off the main square of old Jaffa, with the Turkish clock tower in its centre. A few yards along this road from the square stands a mosque. It was built in 1810, but it is of mild archaeological interest because some of its pillars were constructed from sections of Roman columns brought from the ruins of Caesarea.

On the other side of the road and a little way up the hill is an excellent archaeological museum devoted to the history and antiquities of Tel Aviv-Jaffa.

RAMLA

Ramla is one of the few towns in the country with several well preserved Moslem and Crusader relics yet with no previous history. By Israel standards it is indeed a "new" town, being not more than twelve hundred and fifty years old. It was established by the Moslems — the only town, in fact, built by them in Palestine. It was founded in the year 716 A.D. by the caliph Suleiman, son of the celebrated Abd al-Malik, the Umayyad caliph who erected the Moslem shrine in Jerusalem, the original Dome of the Rock.

The establishment of Ramla seems somewhat strange at first sight. For in those days, a new city was usually developed upon the ruins of an earlier settlement which, in its turn, had been raised on a particular site for good reason. Ramla however was built on a virgin tract of sand, innocent of any previous habitation. Its very name stems from this fact: Ramla, in Arabic, means "the sandy". What was the "good reason" for its establishment? And if the reason was good, why had no earlier people founded a city on this spot?

Ramla owes its establishment largely to its location. It commanded the junction of two great caravan routes — the south-north route from Egypt to Syria and Mesopotamia, and the west-east route from the Mediterranean coast to the interior. Indeed, Ramla today is the most "passed through" town in Israel, lying astride the main Tel Aviv-Jerusalem highway, a half hour's drive southeast from the coast, and roughly midway along the road from Beersheba to Haifa. Why, then, was there no settlement at so strategic a spot before the 8th Century? The fact is that there was such a settlement to carry out these strategic functions sited only a short distance away. This was the very ancient city of Lod (Lydda), close to the modern international airport, which lies three miles to the northeast of Ramla. In about the year 700, Lod was sacked by a Moslem army, led, it is believed, by the very Suleiman who was later to become caliph and who at the time was serving as a general in his father's forces. When he ascended the throne in 715, he saw the strategic necessity of a town in this neighbourhood. Since he, alone of the caliphs, decided to make Palestine his country of residence, he resolved to build himself a new capital on a new site. Ramla, close to the road junction and to old Lod, was the site he chose. There he built himself a palace and a large mosque.

There is now no trace of his palace, destroyed no doubt during the bitter battles later fought between the Saracens and the Crusaders. But fragmentary relics of his mosque, rebuilt by Saladin at the end of the 12th Century, are to be seen today on the open ground a few hundred yards behind the police station on the main road, at the foot of the "White Tower", Ramla's most spectacular landmark. They include a small part of the eastern section of the shrine, the remains of a fountain, and a tomb. Three stone staircases in the now open mosque compound lead to three, large, underground halls, also probably 8th Century, and it is possible that they, too, were part of the structures associated with the original mosque. Two have already been cleared and excavations are continuing in the third, showing them to be in a fine state of preservation. All three have high vaulted ceilings which rest on stout pillars of stone. They are grouped round a square-shaped cistern with arched bays.

The ruins at the southern and eastern ends of the mosque compound, standing at ground level, belong to a later period. They are part of a mediaeval inn which served the caravans on the main trunk highways and also pilgrims on their way to Jerusalem.

The lofty, square, six-storey tower that rises 90 feet above the mosque ruins was built in the second half of the 13th Century as a minaret to Suleiman's 8th Century Moslem shrine. It is known both as the "White Tower" and as the "Tower of the Forty Martyrs" — a name of obscure origin. For a long time it was believed to have been built in the 14th Century because of the 1318 date inscribed on its lintel. Most scholars, however, are now agreed that it was originally constructed by the sultan Baibars when he reconquered Ramla from the Crusaders in 1268. It was probably repaired at the later date.

Underground vaults and cistern, possibly. 8th Century A.D.

It is a graceful and compact structure, its four faces adorned by arched windows and its corners buttressed by elegant columns. The top of the tower, reached by a spiral staircase, commands a view of the coastal strip to the west, and, to the southeast, the Vale of Ayalon, where Joshua bade the moon stand still. It was from here that Napoleon is said to have surveyed the progress of his army's successful attack on Jaffa in 1799 when he was fighting his way northwards, little dreaming as he did so that only a few months' later, his debacle at Acre would render his efforts at Jaffa superfluous.

What is known as the Great Mosque is a few hundred yards to the east of the "White Tower", at the back of what is now the market place of Ramla. This rectangular building was originally a Crusader church, constructed in the 12th Century. It is the largest and one of the best preserved Crusader buildings in the country, and its interior is far more impressive than its dowdy outside would suggest. The formidable domed nave is divided from its vaulted aisles by two series of huge columns whose capitals also serve as springers to decorative arches. It is an expression of the power, ingenuity and grace of Crusader architecture.

To its immediate west is the Franciscan monastery which for centuries offered shelter to pilgrims who often had to wait in Ramla until permission, frequently delayed, was granted to them to enter Jerusalem. It is called the Hospice of St. Joseph of Arimathea because of the not very well based but strongly held mediaeval Christian tradition that Ramla was the Arimathea of the man who besought from Pilate the body of Jesus for burial. Napoleon used this monastery for a brief period as his staff headquarters.

On the other side of the main road and to the immediate north of the monastery is a beautifully constructed cistern, possibly belonging to the 8th Century. The name given to it by mediaeval Christian pilgrims, who refreshed themselves by its waters in the middle of sandy Ramla, was the Pool of St. Helena — after the mother of Constantine. The debris of centuries has now been cleared and the cistern is once again partially filled with water. An ancient stone staircase leads to its base from which giant columns rise to form twenty-four arched bays, each with an aperture in its dome which is now glassed in. A small boat now awaits visitors at the bottom of the steps, and in it one can paddle between the columns to inspect the interesting stonework round the bays. It is believed that in the 8th Century, this cistern was linked by conduit to the one beneath Suleiman's mosque, only a few hundred yards away to the southwest.

11th Century documents mention the Jewish community of Ramla. It is known that Jews lived in this town for a considerable period during the Middle Ages, together with significant communities of Karaites and Samaritans.

LOD (LYDDA)

Lod, in the intervals between its successive destructions, enjoyed a modest strategic and commercial importance for something like two thousand years before it was wiped out by the Moslems at the beginning of the 8th Century A.D. and replaced by the new town of Ramla. It was indeed a very old city, in existence already in the days of Joshua — a walled city according to Talmudic tradition. Its name at that time was Lod, and so it is called in the Old Testament record of its having been built by the offspring of Benjamin (I Chronicles VIII, 12). More than a thousand years later, it was known as Lydda, and this name appears in the New Testament report of St. Peter's miraculous cure of the sick man Aeneas (Acts IX, 32). With the establishment of the State of Israel in 1948, the earlier Biblical name was revived.

Lod shared the fate of the other cities of Judah in the 6th Century B.C. Babylonian conquest, and its inhabitants were carried off into exile. With the Jewish return, it was soon resettled and the fact is noted in the Books of Ezra (II, 33) and Nehemiah (VII, 37). Some 350 years later, the great rebellion of the Maccabees was touched off in a village in the foothills only a few miles to the east of Lod, the village of Modin. In the year 143 B.C., the district of Lod was incorporated into the area under Hasmonean rule.

In the 66–70 A.D. war of the Jews against the Romans, Lod was reduced by the forces who were on their way to attack and destroy Jerusalem. In the next Century, however, it was gradually resettled and became renowned as a seat of Jewish learning, with an academy graced by prominent sages, including Rabbi Eleazar ben Hyrcanus and Rabbi Tarfon. The renowned Rabbi Akiva, zealous supporter of Bar Kochba, also lived there for a while. In the year 200 A.D., during the visit to the country of the Roman emperor Septimius Severus, Lod was accorded special rights and the city was renamed Diospolis, the name by which it was also known officially in Byzantine times, though the local inhabitants continued to refer to it as Lod. In the year 351, after a series of Jewish outbreaks against tyrannical authority, the army of emperor Constantinus II took harsh action against the community, including the deliberate destruction of their main centres of learning — Tiberias, Sepphoris and Lod.

Archaeological items from ancient Lod include a Jewish tomb with ossuaries, and a Greco-Samaritan inscription. There are also remains of Byzantine and Crusader masonry — and there is a strange legend. Just off today's High Street is a Greek Orthodox church adjoining a mosque. Both stand on the ruins of a 12th Century Crusader basilica which in turn was erected on the ruins of a 6th Century Byzantine church. The church is an 1870 restoration of part of the Crusader structure and contains the original pillars, arches and apse. It is called

Mameluke bridge near Lod, 13th Century A.D.

the Church of St. George, the patron saint of England who is always depicted as a mediaeval knight slaying the dragon. Legend has it that he was born in Lod, served as a Roman legionary, became a Christian, was put to death for his faith at the beginning of the 4th Century, and was buried in his native town. How this legendary figure became identified with the legendary dragon-slayer is a mystery. How he became transformed into a mediaeval knight and absorbed into English mythology is less mysterious. He was almost certainly brought to England on the tongues of returning Crusaders.

North of Lod, the main road to the international airport crosses a stone bridge. This is a restoration of a late 13th Century bridge built by the Mamelukes. This fact — and the 1278 date — are recorded in the Arabic inscription on the stone slab between the two sculptured lions set above the arch.

ABU GHOSH

The road from Tel Aviv on the coast to Jerusalem in the Judean hills covers the first 30 miles across level plain and then begins its sharp ascent at "The Gate to the Valley" — Shaar Hagai in Hebrew, Bab el Wad in Arabic. For the next 5½ miles it winds its way upwards through a huge mountain cleft between steep pine-covered slopes. Emerging from the gorge, it skirts a village which seems to grow out of the hillside. This is Abu Ghosh. From here the traveller gains his first glimpse of Jerusalem, 7½ miles away to the east; and so pious Jewish pilgrims used to rend their garments at this spot, in mourning over the destruction of the Temple.

The name, Abu Ghosh, is comparatively new; the site of the village is old, its first settlement going back to the Chalcolithic Age in the 4th millennium B.C. In Biblical times, here stood Kiriat Ye'arim, where the Ark of the Covenant rested for many years after its recovery from the Philistines and before David brought it to Jerusalem. Kiriat Ye'arim is Hebrew for "City of Forests" — which is what it was in ancient days before the neglect of man and the greed of goats left the countryside denuded. Trees have now been planted and grow once again on the Judean slopes.

Kiriat Ye'arim continued as a lively settlement in Israelite times until the destruction of the First Temple and the Jewish exile to Babylon in the 6th Century B.C. With the return of the Jews it was resettled and lasted some six hundred years.

The village of Abu Ghosh.

It then suffered the same fate as Jerusalem, being destroyed when the Second Temple was destroyed and the great Jewish revolt crushed. For some time thereafter, a unit of the Tenth Roman Legion was stationed here. The Byzantines who followed left their imprint on the village by building a church on the summit of the hill on the northern side of the main road (where now stands the church of the Vierge Marie Arche d'Alliance with its dominating figure of the Madonna and Child). The Crusaders in their day built a more formidable basilica over the spring at the entrance to the village, on the southern side of the highway. It is the best-preserved Crusader church in the country.

The site was settled in the 18th Century by the clan of Abu Ghosh, believed to have stemmed from a bedouin tribe in Arabia. So powerful did they become and so entrenched was their influence in the region that the former names of this settlement were forgotten and the village came to be known by the name of the clan. 19th Century travellers to the Holy Land have recorded grim tales of Christian pilgrims en route to Jerusalem having to run the gauntlet at Abu Ghosh. Those lucky enough to escape being plundered were forced to pay a levy before being allowed to pass, on pain of dire physical penalty. Abu Ghosh today is a peaceful and flourishing Arab village. It was the only one in the area during Israel's War of Independence which did not take part in attacks against the Jews. Indeed, a number of the villagers joined one of the Jewish underground movements in Mandatory days. They now live on the friendliest terms with their Jewish neighbours.

The most impressive archaeological remains at Abu Ghosh are those of the Crusader church. It passed into the hands of the French government in the second half of the last century and was assigned to the Benedictine Fathers who carried out a restoration of the ruins and added a small monastery in 1899. The church was part of a Crusader castle built by the Order of Hospitalers and known both as the Castle of the Spring and the Castle of Emmaus. They believed this to be the New Testament site of "a village called Emmaus, which was from Jerusalem about threescore furlongs", mentioned by St. Luke as having been visited by Jesus three days after the crucifixion. (xxiv, 13).

This church is smaller and more austere than the one in Ramla; but its architectural design is of noble proportions and its masonry and massive interior columns give the same impression of structural power. The ceilings of its nave and aisles are flat, and instead of columns along the walls there are stone projections to carry the arches. Its sole decoration consisted of frescoes on the walls. Adjoining the church are a Crusader hall and a refectory. Powerful arches support the huge crypt below the church, containing the spring which prompted the Crusaders to choose this site for their shrine.

A stone tablet set in the wall of the church is inscribed with the Latin original of "Detachment of the Tenth Legion". The tablet belonged to a building put up by the Roman garrison which occupied this site more than one thousand years earlier.

The hilltop church with the Madonna was erected in 1924 by the French Sisters of St. Joseph on what they believe to have been the very spot in Biblical Kiriat Ye'arim where the Ark rested. It stands on the foundations of a larger, 5th Century A.D., Byzantine church, and some of the original columns and stonework were used in the construction of the present building. Parts of Byzantine mosaics are to be seen in the floors of church and courtyard. A small chapel near the altar is held by some to be the site of a 2nd Century B.C. Hasmonean structure. Its floor is lower than the Byzantine level and it is decorated with a well-preserved early mosaic, different in pattern and stone from the Christian mosaics. Strewn about the compound are ornamental capitals, bases and fragments of columns belonging to the Byzantine, Roman and even earlier periods. On the slope some fifty yards from the summit are the relics of Canaanite settlement.

ASHKELON

Ashkelon is Israel's southernmost town on the Mediterranean coast and, like Jaffa and Acre, it is the site of one of the oldest cities in the world. Its ancient location is the artificial mound that rises above the shore to the immediate south of newly built Afridar-Ashkelon, the neatly planned garden city with its red gabled cottages and green lawns that reach down to the sandy beach. It is an hour's drive from Tel Aviv and from Jerusalem. Within the mound, or archaeological Tell, lie buried the remains of six levels of early settlement, each city having been built upon the ruins of its predecessor — Canaanite, Philistine, Graeco-Roman, Byzantine, Moslem and Crusader.

In ancient times Ashkelon was a port of some importance, its harbour sited at the mouth of a stream which broke through the low cliffs skirting the shore. In the centuries since its abandonment, the harbour has silted up and the coastline is now virtually unbroken. Before that time, Ashkelon was largely a trading town, though engaging, too, in agriculture. Today it is a modest centre of farming and light industry, and an attractive holiday resort. Husbandry is thus a feature common to the environs of both the old and the new Ashkelon. Blessed by sun and sweet water springs, the soil in this region is very fertile, with fruits and

vegetables growing in profusion. Indeed, two thousand years ago, during the Roman period, the vineyards and gardens of Ashkelon were noted for their luxuriance, and Ashkelon wine was exported to France and Italy. It was the Romans who popularised the onion of Ashkelon — "caepa Ascalonia" — from which the modern scallion and shallot take their names.

This fertility, allied to its topography and strategic location, were the prime reasons for Ashkelon's early importance. Topographic conditions made possible the building of a city right on the coast, unlike neighbouring Gaza and Ashdod which developed at some distance from their ports. It enjoyed a rich agricultural, and therefore a densely populated, hinterland. It was close to the busy international caravan route from Egypt in the south to Syria and Mesopotamia in the north — the Sea Road, and it commanded an easy route into the interior of the country. Small wonder that rival peoples and empires should have battled for its possession for so many centuries.

Archaeological excavations carried out just over forty years ago show that the first Ashkelon was established at the end of the 3rd millennium B.C. and was already a city of some importance by the beginning of the 2nd millennium. It was one of the Canaanite cities recorded in the 19th Century B.C. Execration Texts, when Egypt was at the height of its early imperial power. These texts were a Pharaonic device to exercise political witchcraft — an early form of psychological warfare — against the actual or potential enemies of Egypt. In the 19th Century group of texts, the names of such enemies and imprecations against them were inscribed on bowls; in the later, 18th Century texts, they were written on clay

Bronze figurine from a hoard found at Ashkelon, probably 4th Century B.C.

figurines representing bound captives. Smashing the bowl or figurine was held to make the imprecation effective. Or it may be that the knowledge, by a potential foe, that it was in the power of the pharaoh to do him harm by violent execration, was sufficient to keep him friendly to Egypt. At all events, these texts, by including the names of vassal rulers and cities marked down for possible execration, reveal the extent of Egypt's sphere of influence in those days. In the early Execration Texts we find "the ruler of Asqaluni (Ashkelon) Khalukim and all the retainers who are with him. . ."

With the Hyksos invasion of the country in the 18th Century, the city of Ashkelon fell to new masters who were to remain in occupation for some two hundred years. The excavations showed that the Hyksos conquerors fortified the city by surrounding it with a bank of beaten earth.

From the 15th to the 13th Centuries B.C. the country came once again under Egyptian tutelage. The Canaanite princes were answerable to the local Egyptian governor though they could send a direct address to the pharaoh. A record of some of their activities has come down to us precisely though such addresses, found in that archaeological treasure, the Tell el-Amarna archives of the pharaohs

Amenhotep III and IV. From these letters we learn something of Ashkelon and her relations both with her rulers and with her neighbours at the beginning of the 14th Century B.C.

As a vassal city-state, Ashkelon paid tribute to Egypt. Here are extracts from typical letters sent by an Ashkelon prince to the pharaoh: "To the king, my pantheon, my Sun-god, the Sun-god of heaven: Thus Widia, the prince of Ashkelon, thy servant, the dirt under thy feet, the groom of thy horse. At the feet of the king, my lord, seven times and seven times verily I fall, both prone and supine. Now I am guarding the place of the king which is with me, and whatever the king, my lord, has sent to me I have heard very attentively. Who is the dog that does not hearken to the words of the king ... Verily, I have prepared everything possible that the king, my lord, has commanded. Behold I have prepared it. And behold I prepare the tribute of the sun according as the king, my lord, the sun in heaven, has commanded."

It is unlikely, however, that the pharaoh missed the smirk beneath the unction. For following on the heels of this fulsome missive, and also found in the el-Amarna archives, is a despatch from the Egyptian governor in Jerusalem reporting to pharaoh that the people of Ashkelon have been secretly supplying food to the enemies of Egypt.

This was the fairly common practice of vassal states — in olden as in modern times. Disaffection would occasionally erupt into outright rebellion. As with other cities under Egyptian rule, Ashkelon revolted several times against colonial authority. One such rebellion at the beginning of the 13th Century B.C. is commemorated in a contemporary relief discovered in the ruins of Karnak in Upper Egypt. It was carved on one of the walls of the palace of Rameses II in about the year 1280. It shows Egyptian troops breaking through the fortifications of Ashkelon and depicts some Ashkelonites with arms raised in supplication or surrender and others in the act of being killed. The caption to the relief reads: "The wretched town, which His Majesty took when it was wicked, Ashkelon."

The conquest of Ashkelon by another Egyptian king, pharaoh Marniptah, in about the year 1225 is noted on a stele which is of considerable importance to archaeologists. For the inscription on this 13th Century upright slab of stone contains the earliest reference to Israel in a contemporary record. It lists the cities and peoples conquered by Marniptah: "... Carried off is Ashkelon; seized upon is Gezer ... Israel is laid waste, his seed is not ..."

In the second half of the 12th Century B.C. Egyptian imperial power, already beginning to decline since the end of the previous century, received its death blow by the attacks of the "Sea Peoples", among them the Philistines. When they invaded the Egyptian colonial territory of Canaan, the pharaoh lacked the strength to eject them. The Philistines settled along the coast and established five important cities, of which Ashkelon was one. (The others were Gath, Gaza, Ashdod and Ekron). Archaeological excavations show that they utterly destroyed the Ashkelon of the Canaanites and built a new city, reflecting a vastly different and more advanced material culture.

A generation or two earlier, the Israelites had entered the country from the east, arriving from Transjordan and settling in the interior of the country. A clash was inevitable with the new arrivals who were now in occupation of the coastal strip. Indeed, the Philistines with their new iron weapons and their tight social and military organisation caused much harassment to the Israelites. Throughout the entire period of the Judges there was constant warfare between the two peoples, the Philistines seeking to extend their territory and put the Israelites under bondage.

The Israelite leader most closely associated with the region of Ashkelon during this period is Samson. His final act when, as a prisoner, he killed three thousand of the enemy by tearing down the temple pillars, crying "Let me die with the Philistines", occurred in nearby Gaza. The Bible records that when he was a young man, "the Spirit of the Lord came upon him, and he went down to Ashkelon, and slew thirty men of them, and took their spoil..." (Judges xiv, 19).

It was under David that Israel scored its major successes against the Philistines, but it was his predecessor, Saul, Israel's first king, who struck the preliminary significant blows against this enemy, even though he was to die at their hands on the battlefield. The record of this event provided Ashkelon with its most memorable mention in the Scriptures — in David's lament over the death of Saul and Jonathan: "Tell it not in Gath, publish it not in the streets of Ashkelon; lest the daughters of the Philistines rejoice, lest the daughters of the uncircumcised triumph." (II Samuel i, 20.)

Some two hundred years later, the prophet Amos thunders: "And I will cut off ... him that holdeth the sceptre of Ashkelon ... and the remnant of the Philistines shall perish, saith the Lord God." (Amos i, 8.) About one hundred and fifty years after Amos, Zephaniah prophesies that the Philistines will be conquered and their cities occupied by the Israelites: "And the coast shall be for the remnant of the house of Judah ... in the houses of Ashkelon shall they lie down in the evening..." (Zephaniah ii, 7.) (Not surprisingly, the main thoroughfare in modern Ashkelon is named Zephaniah Boulevard).

There are records of tribute paid by Ashkelon to the empires which successively overran the country, the Assyrians, the Babylonians, the Persians. During the Hellenistic period that followed, Ashkelon flourished as a commercial centre, and among the ruins visible on the site today are statues recovered from the Greek temples of those days. It continued its prosperity under the Romans, Herod in

particular adorning the city with fine buildings. Josephus wrote that at Ashkelon Herod built "waterworks, baths, and large and beautiful piazzas and cloisters." Under Byzantium Ashkelon became a Christian city, though the Jews were the only minority community allowed to practise their religion and maintain a synagogue. It continued as a settled city after the Moslem conquest right up to the end of the Crusades. The Crusaders had a hard time trying to reduce Ashkelon, but it finally fell to Baldwin III in 1153 A.D. We know something of its life a little after this time from the chronicle of the Jewish traveller Benjamin of Tudela who visited Ashkelon in 1171, describing it as "a very large and handsome city; and merchants from all parts resort to it, on account of its convenient situation on the confines of Egypt. There are about two hundred Jews . . ."

In the next hundred years Ashkelon changed hands several times, until it was ultimately destroyed by the sultan Baibars in 1270 A.D. The city was demolished and abandoned. Nor was there any attempt at its rehabilitation after the Turkish conquest of the country in 1517, though in the 19th Century Ibrahim Pasha ordered a fort to be built on the seashore. Among the materials used for this Turkish fort were Crusader masonry and parts of marble columns, floor slabs and statues taken from the Greek and Roman ruins. Only with the establishment of the State of Israel in 1948, almost seven centuries after Baibars' destruction, was Ashkelon rebuilt and resettled.

The antiquities of Ashkelon are now easily accessible since the Department for Landscaping and the Preservation of Historic Sites completed a tasteful landscaping programme in 1960, clearing the wild foliage, laying out lawns and footpaths, partially restoring some of the ruins and offering them the setting of a modest national park.

Most of the ruins and relics within the park are Hellenistic, Roman and Byzantine, discovered during the excavations carried out in 1920–21 by the British archaeologists J. Garstang and P. Adams on behalf of the Palestine Exploration Fund. This was the main area of their dig. They then discovered that the site of Biblical Ashkelon was the artificial mound that rises just beyond what is now the southern end of the park, covering an area of fifteen acres. They found this by carrying out a trial sounding on the Tell, enough to allow them to examine the artefacts and see something of construction techniques in each stratum, and to establish that settlements on this spot ranged from the period of the Patriarchs to that of the Philistines. The remains of the embankment of beaten earth near the Tell are parts of the Hyksos fortifications.

The western slope of the mound reaches down to the beach and is bounded by the ruins of an ancient sea-wall with columns sticking out of it like the barrels of coastal guns. The columns are Roman. The wall belongs to a later date, probably

Byzantine. The columns were certainly used to strengthen the wall and give greater protection to the harbour area from the pounding of the sea. A thorough excavation of this Tell is likely to yield fruitful finds from the early periods of settlement in Ashkelon.

Within the park compound, the centre of archaeological interest is the collection of Hellenistic and Roman statues, columns, capitals and inscribed and decorated marble slabs grouped in what looks like a sunken court at the end of the eastern lawn, a few hundred yards from the entrance. The "court" itself is part of a Herodian building, and some of the columns and capitals belong to the colonnaded structures also built by Herod, as recorded by Josephus.

The most interesting of the sculptured figures are the winged goddess of victory — Nike — standing upon a globe of the world which rests upon the shoulders of Atlas; a goddess bearing a palm branch; and a goddess and child — Isis and Harpocrates. The relics also include tablets from ancient synagogues with inscriptions in Hebrew.

Towering on the high ground above this eastern rim of the park are huge sections of the solid stone wall built by the Crusaders.

About a mile north of the park, close to the main beach of modern Ashkelon, is a 3rd Century A.D. tomb, discovered by chance some years ago. It was apparently the burial chamber of a wealthy pagan Roman family, and is embellished with coloured frescos on the well-plastered walls and vaulted ceiling. The architecture and painting are a good example of art styles at the end of the Roman empire. Two nymphs beside the bank of a stream adorn the wall facing the entrance. The fresco on the ceiling is an intricate pattern of vine-branches with leaves and grape-clusters; these are woven round mythological characters, to drive away evil spirits, and pastoral vignettes, symbolic of life in the Hereafter, which include a youth harvesting grapes, a feeding gazelle, a hound chasing a doe, and the shepherd god Pan playing an eight-reed pipe.

LACHISH, MARESHAH, BETH GOVRIN

Twenty miles inland from Ashkelon lies the site of the celebrated Biblical city of Lachish, subject of the remarkable 8th Century B.C. battle scenes in stone relief which adorned the palace of Sennacherib in Nineveh (and which are now in the

British Museum) and the location which yielded to the excavator's spade the important 6th Century B.C. "Lachish Letters". It is five miles southeast of another ancient Tell, believed to hold the remains of Philistine Ashkelon's sister city, Gath, close to the new township which bears its name, Kiriat Gath.

Excavations at Lachish (Tell ed-Duweir) were carried out by the Wellcome-Marston Expedition directed by the archaeologist J.L. Starkey from 1932 until his murder by Arab brigands in 1938. He uncovered nine levels of settlement, the earliest dating back to the middle of the 3rd millennium B.C. The 18th to 16th Centuries B.C. strata revealed the hand of the Hyksos conquerors. They had fortified the city and built their characteristic steep embankment round it, with a moat at the bottom. They were well aware of its strategic importance — as were the armies of later empires — guarding as it did the approaches to the Judean hills and to Jerusalem from the south, and, from the north, the route to Egypt.

In the late Canaanite level — end of the 13th Century B.C. — the archaeologists found the remains of a city, including a temple, which had been violently destroyed, evidently by the Israelites. "And Joshua passed from Libna, and all Israel with him, unto Lachish, and encamped against it, and fought against it: And the Lord delivered Lachish into the hand of Israel, which took it on the second day, and smote it with the edge of the sword . . ." (Joshua x, 31–32.)

Early in the 10th Century B.C. David made it a provincial administrative centre. His grandson, Rehoboam, in about the year 920 B.C., strengthened its defences — the remains of double walls with towers encircling the city, found by the excavators, probably belong to this period — and provisioned it with food and weapons to enable it to withstand a long siege. "And Rehoboam . . . built cities for defence in Judah. He built even Bethlehem . . . and Gath, and Mareshah . . . and Lachish . . . And he fortified the strongholds, and put captains in them, and store of victual, and of oil and wine. And in every several city he put shields and spears, and made them exceeding strong . . ." (II Chronicles XI, 5–12.)

In 701 B.C. came the most noted of all the battles of Lachish when the Assyrian emperor Sennacherib, after conquering several cities in Judah — but not Jerusalem — found his way to Egypt blocked. Following a siege of Lachish, his men stormed its ramparts and in violent fighting overwhelmed the Jewish defenders. His casualties, too, must have been heavy, for found in the excavations at the stratum of that period were numerous Assyrian weapons and bronze helmets. When Sennacherib returned home, he ordered his war artists to decorate the walls of his palace at Nineveh (Kuyunjuk) with bas-reliefs depicting the highlights of his campaign. The battle scenes of Lachish were among them. They were found by the British archaeologist Layard in 1847, and are most illuminating on

Interior of Beth Govrin caves, believed to be result of ancient quarrying.

the type of weapons, the nature of fortifications and the art of warfare in defence and assault of those days.

Just over one hundred years later, the resettled Lachish was partly destroyed in the first invasion of Judah by Nebuchadnezzar, king of Babylon, (598–597 B.C.), and completely destroyed in his second invasion (587 B.C.). In the period level between these two actions, among the burnt debris in a chamber of the city gate, Starkey made the remarkable discovery of 18 ostraca — inscribed potsherds — in early Hebrew script. Three more were later found elsewhere on the site. The classical Hebrew prose was written in black ink on broken pottery vessels. They are for the most part reports written in the year 589 or 588 B.C. by the liaison officer between Lachish and Jerusalem to the commander of the Lachish fortress, one of the last Judean cities to fall to the Babylonians before the conquest of Jerusalem. They reflect the pessimism evident in Jeremiah when Zedekiah, the last king of Judah, had him brought from prison and "asked him secretly in his house, and said, Is there any word from the Lord? And Jeremiah said, There is: for, said he, thou shalt be delivered into the hand of the king of Babylon." (XXXVII, 17.)

On the return of the Jews from Babylonian exile, Lachish was resettled. New fortifications were erected and a new palace was built on the ruins of the old. The remains of this structure, belonging to the 5th Century B.C., may be seen on the summit of the mound. After the 4th Century B.C., Lachish declined in importance when the administrative centre was moved to nearby Mareshah. With the Roman destruction of Jerusalem and the great exile of the Jews from the country, Lachish fell into ruins and the Tell remains a ruin to this day, though the surrounding area has been revived by the pioneers of modern Israel, and bears its name.

The location of Biblical Mareshah, one of the cities mentioned with Lachish as having been fortified by Rehoboam, is a conspicuous Tell some three miles northeast of Lachish. The site was positively identified in archaeological excavations undertaken in 1898–1900. (Incidentally, several stamped jar handles in early Hebrew script were found at the time.) In the Hellenistic period it was known as Marissa. During the Hasmonean reign, the Idumeans, who had by then penetrated into the area and made Mareshah their capital, were engaged by the forces of Judah the Maccabee. They were finally subdued by Judah's nephew, John Hyrcanus, who regained Mareshah towards the end of the 2nd Century B.C. Pompey, shortly after the Roman occupation in 63 B.C., built it anew, but it was soon destroyed by the Parthians in their war with Herod.

In Crusader times, Mareshah was a monastic outpost, and a Crusader basilica was built in the 12th or 13th Century A.D. whose ruins may be seen a few hundred yards to the east of the Tell. It was called the Church of St. Anna, and this is the source of "Sandanna", the local name by which Mareshah was known until quite recently.

The most important remains unearthed by the excavations are the foundations of the 2nd Century B.C. city, the ruins of its walls, towers, streets, market place and houses. The archaeologists found enough to enable them to prepare a detailed town plan of Mareshah as it was then. They also found several water cisterns scooped out of the hill; a fine columbarium, with its tiers of burial niches; and two large burial caves, one of them with Greek inscriptions and decorative paintings on the walls.

One of the "Lachish Letters", written on a potsherd in the year 589 B.C. in early Hebrew script.

A mile north of Tell Mareshah, hard by the Ashkelon-Hartuv road, is the site of ancient Beth Govrin. (The new kibbutz which bears its name is a short distance away.) Beth Govrin rose to prominence in the Roman period. Before then it had been little more than a village, playing no major defensive role in the area. This function, as we have seen, had fallen first to Lachish and later to Mareshah. By the beginning of the 3rd Century A.D., however, there was no fortress in the region to command the important road junction. The emperor Septimius Severus, visiting his eastern domains at the time, promptly decided to establish one.

Instead of building on the ruins of neighbouring Lachish and Mareshah, he ordered that Beth Govrin be converted into a fortified city, made it an administrative centre and added considerable lands to its possessions. At this time, its population was largely gentile, but it also had its Jewish community. Excavations revealed the ruins of a synagogue, with a seven-branched candelabrum sculptured on the capital of one of its columns. Another column bore a Hebrew inscription. (Most of the relics of this 3rd Century synagogue are now in the Rockefeller Museum in the old city of Jerusalem).

There is a fine mosaic of the Roman period, with pastoral and hunting scenes, which is on display in Jerusalem. But in two period levels above the spot where it was found were two more mosaic floors, with a motif of birds and animals, and these may be seen on the site. They are Byzantine, belonging to the 5th and 6th Centuries. These mosaics are at the top of the hill and a protective hut has now been built over them. (The key is kept in the nearby kibbutz).

Beth Govrin fell to the Crusaders at the beginning of the 12th Century A.D. and they built up its fortifications and added a citadel. Their structures were largely destroyed by Saladin, but the remains of one Crusader building have been preserved to this day. These are the ruins seen near the road.

BEERSHEBA

At the beginning of this century, Beersheba, evocative of the slow pastoral life in bygone ages, was nothing more than a name in the pages of the Bible. It no longer existed as a site of habitation, having been abandoned hundreds of years earlier. Then the Turkish authorities built a small administrative and marketing centre for the local bedouin near the spot where the ancient city had stood. When General Allenby's Australian cavalry captured it in 1917, they found it a sand-swept desert village with a population of barely two thousand. Thirty-one years later, when it fell to the Israel army in the Arab-Jewish war, its population had grown by no more than one thousand. Today it is the capital of the Negev, with scores of thousands of busy inhabitants who have themselves laid the roads and parks and built their sprawling housing estates, and government offices which administer the entire southern district of the country. It has important industries based on Negev raw materials; it serves the Negev's agricultural settlements; and it is Israel's southern railhead and road transport centre. But this modern urban phenomenon planted in the desert acquires a colourful Biblical look every Thursday morning, market day for the surrounding bedouin, who come in with their camels and donkeys and their exotic desert ware to bargain and haggle in the time-worn manner of the East.

It is on such days in particular that Beersheba is recalled as one of the best known of the Old Testament sites, closely bound up with the lives of the Patriarchs. In their day, Beersheba was neither city nor fortress nor major gateway. It was simply a cluster of wells in the open desert. But these were a blessing to their flocks, and the Patriarchs made it a sanctuary. Abraham planted a tamarisk there, "and called there on the name of the Lord, the everlasting God" (Genesis XXI, 33). Isaac "builded an altar there, and called upon the name of the Lord" (Genesis XXVI, 25). Jacob pitched his tent there, and shortly after "he went out from Beersheba" (XXVIII, 10) had his dream of the ladder leading to Heaven and his vision of God.

Beersheba is Hebrew for "Well of the Oath", the oath sworn by Abraham and Abimelech when they made their covenant: "And Abraham took sheep and oxen, and gave them unto Abimelech; and both of them made a covenant. And Abraham set seven ewe lambs of the flock by themselves ... And he said, For these ewe lambs shalt thou take of my hand, that they may be a witness unto me, that I have digged this well. Wherefore he called that place Beersheba; because there they sware both of them." (Genesis XXI, 27–31.)

In those days Beersheba with its water wells must have served as a small wayside station for caravans plying one of the trade routes between Canaan and Egypt and the Arabian peninsula. In the context of the times, it was of sufficient impor-

Ivory head found in Beersheba excavations, Chalcolithic period.

tance to have been mentioned in the tribal allocations which followed Joshua's conquest of the country. It fell within the area assigned to the tribe of Simeon. It was then considered the southernmost city in the land, and "north to south" was more tangibly expressed as "from Dan to Beersheba" (II Samuel III, 10).

It must have become some kind of religious and administrative district centre in the time of Samuel (11th Century B.C.), for he sent his two sons, Joel and Abiah, to sit in judgement there: "And it came to pass, when Samuel was old, that he made his sons judges over Israel . . . they were judges in Beersheba" (I Samuel VIII, 1,2). But the next verse tells us that the appointment turned out badly, for "his sons walked not in his ways, but turned aside after lucre . . . and perverted judgement". Their corruption in Beersheba, indeed, sparked the popular demand for a monarchy, the people coming to Samuel and crying: "Behold, thou art old, and thy sons walk not in thy ways: now make us a king to judge us like all the nations." The result was the crowning of Saul.

Beersheba is next mentioned in the Bible as the place where the prophet Elijah, in the 9th Century B.C., sought refuge from the wrath of queen Jezebel, the dominating pagan wife of king Ahab. When her husband had told her how Elijah had slain four hundred prophets of Baal, Jezebel promptly vowed to make Elijah's life "as the life of one of them by tomorrow about this time". Whereupon Elijah, taking advantage of the twenty-four hours' notice, "arose, and went for his life, and came to Beersheba, which belongeth to Judah" (I Kings XIX, 2,3). This was already the period of the divided monarchy, when Israel and Judah were separate states. By fleeing to Beersheba, Elijah was beyond the jurisdiction of Israel authority.

When the Jews returned from captivity in Babylon in the 6th Century B.C., Beersheba was one of the places they resettled, and it soon became once again a station on the caravan route to Egypt and Arabia. It appears in the long and detailed list of towns and villages recorded in the Book of Nehemiah as having been revived by the returning Jews: "And for the villages, with their fields, some of the children of Judah dwelt at Kirjath-arba . . . and at Beersheba, and in the villages thereof . . . And they dwelt from Beersheba unto the valley of Hinnom" (XI, 25, 27, 30).

During the Roman period, a garrison of legionaries was maintained at Beersheba, and it is described in contemporary records as "a very large village."

Until then, the site of Beersheba had always been the Tell which is some three miles to the northeast of the present city. The earliest settlement on the site of today's Beersheba was started in late Roman and early Byzantine times — about the 3rd or 4th Century A.D. Remains have been found of a synagogue built during this period, and parts of the mosaic floor of a Byzantiane church built a

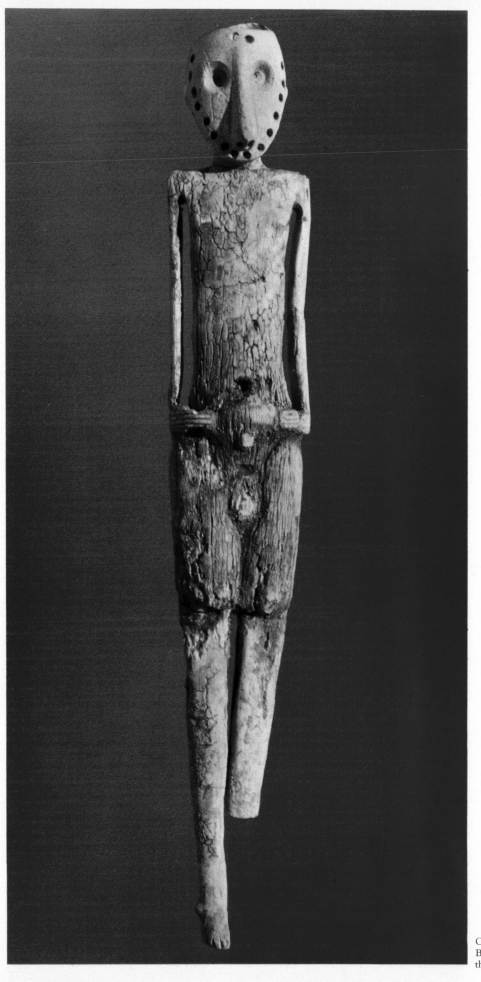

Chalcolithic ivory figurine found near Beersheba. Hair and beard were threaded through holes in jaw and forehead.

little later. The mosaic is on exhibition in the museum of the big mosque, erected by the Turks when they built the new Beersheba early in this century.

The ancient Tell still awaits the spade of the archaeologist to disclose the secrets of the location where Abraham, Isaac, Jacob and later Biblical characters spent part of their lives. There has been only one series of extensive excavations carried out in the Beersheba area, and these were confined to sites just south of the present city. Discovered on these sites were the remains of Chalcolithic settlements whose people had lived here for a relatively brief period in history some fifteen hundred years before the Patriarchs. In 1951, a young member of a neighbouring kibbutz led the French archaeologist, Jean Perrot, to the banks of a wadi where he had found sherds of coarse pottery and flint flakes. A quick inspection convinced Perrot that they were relics of a settlement going back to the 4th millennium B.C. What followed were six seasons of digs at Bir Abu Matar and Bir es-Safadi by Perrot on behalf of the French Centre of Scientific Research, a dig by Dr. Moshe Dothan on behalf of the Israel Department of Antiquities at Khirbet el Bitar, and an excavation by Zvi Ofer, curator of the Beersheba Museum, near Bir el-Ibrahim, the traditional site of the well of Abraham.

Perrot was the first to find the peculiar underground villages of these people in this country. The nature of the soil here favoured such subterranean dwellings, as they offered excellent protection against the sand-borne winds, the heat of the desert day and the chill of the desert night. They were also almost invisible, except close up, to a possible foe. The earliest dwellings of these inhabitants were completely underground and were in the form of large rectangular rooms, no doubt reflecting a tradition of earlier rock-cut shelters in the land of their origin. But these soon crumbled and were replaced by rows of smaller rooms, egg-shaped this time, connected by tunnels and entered by vertical shafts sunk into the end room of each row. The shafts also provided the needed ventilation, and footholds cut in their walls facilitated entry and exit.

These underground villages bore signs of having been abandoned on occasion, possibly owing to drought, the people hiding what they could not carry and smoothing away visible traces of their abodes to make them less conspicuous to possible plunderers. Some of them never returned, and thus left to the archaeologists five thousand years later underground houses complete with furniture and domestic appurtenances. The subterranean settlements later gave way to above-ground living, and the remains of quite sturdy buildings were found at Bir es-Safadi constructed of mud bricks on stone foundations.

The relics provided obvious clues to their economic organisation. It was clearly based on agriculture and cattle raising, and very little on hunting. The finds included farm implements, such as picks, hoes and sickles, made of bone and stone,

Top of bone pin fashioned into a bird, Chalcolithic Period.

and primitive silos containing grains of wheat, barley and lentils. Animal skeletons showed that their flocks were mostly sheep and goats.

Their arts and handicrafts were well developed and often of high standard. Among the finds were graceful pottery vessels, some decorated in colour with geometric designs, and including the characteristic pottery churn of these people; the equally characteristic basalt bowls; weaving and basket work; and ornamental objects and jewellery made of hard stone, bone shell and ivory, including ivory ritual figurines. At Bir es-Safadi, Perrot found intact an ivory carver's workshop, complete with workbench, tools — the copper awl still had its bone handle — and raw material — an elephant tusk. At Bir Abu Matar, he found remains of copper smelting and such copper objects as mace-heads, axes and jewellery.

The pattern of culture of these people is known as Ghassulian. The term comes from the Chalcolithic settlement of Teleilat Ghassul, northeast of the Dead Sea, in Jordan, which was excavated in 1930 by an archaeological expedition of the Pontifical Biblical Institute. Many of the objects found near Beersheba are very similar to those discovered earlier at Teleilat Ghassul (and in the Tel Aviv area). The Beersheba excavations showed that these settlements had suddenly sprung into existence and that their inhabitants, a strange group with a culture special to themselves, had lived there only for a few centuries. They had then vanished as suddenly as they had come. When the Bronze Age began, and roughly until the time of Abraham, the Negev was once again a region of no settled habitation.

MASSADA

To the southeast of Jerusalem, the Judean wilderness rolls eastwards in a bony plateau that ends abruptly after fifteen miles in an escarpment which drops to the edge of a lake. The drop is from 1200 feet above to 1200 feet below sea level. The stretch of water is 50 miles long with an average width of 9 miles, and it covers the lowest section of a gigantic rift that runs from Turkey in the north to the African continent in the south. This lake was called in earliest times the "Sea of Salt". It is better known today as the Dead Sea.

Fed by the southward flowing river Jordan and by the waters of four other streams which are unusually saline, the Dead Sea has no outlet. Evaporation, in the fiery heat at this low altitude, is rapid and constant. The mineral content of the water is thus extraordinarily high. It is made higher by the introduction of other chemicals through hot springs in the sea bottom. The percentage of solids in solution is five times higher than it is in the Atlantic. (So buoyant is the water that a bather cannot drown; whatever his movements, he just floats).

In early Biblical times, the southern edge of this sea was the awesome stage whereon was enacted before primitive man the classic and terrible judgement on human sin. For here stood the cities of Sodom and Gomorrah, upon which "The Lord rained . . . brimstone and fire". (Today's S'dom, which cannot be far from the site of Biblical Sodom, is covered by the largest industrial plant in Israel, the Dead Sea Potash Works, which extracts the rich mineral deposits from the water).

The setting was appropriate for the Biblical drama. The lake, its surface a full-bodied blue, glistening in the hot sun, is bounded in the east by the gaunt mountains of Moab, and in the west by limestone cliffs streaked with marl, looking like the desolate promontories of the moon, rugged, bleak, austere.

Centuries later, the Dead Sea region was the scene of another spectacular event in history, about which more is known through the detailed writings of Josephus. This took place at Massada, an immense rock that rises above the western shore some twenty miles due north of S'dom. It was at Massada that the Jews made their remarkable and tragic last stand for independence against the Romans. Its fall in the year 73 A.D. marked the end of that independence until our own generation, when the State of Israel was proclaimed in 1948.

The rock of Massada projects from the edge of the Judean plateau. Its flat top is shaped like a rhomboid, measuring 650 yards from its northern to its southern points and 216 yards from east to west.

Josephus wrote that Jonathan the High Priest was the first to build a fortress on this rock, and this was long taken to refer to Jonathan Maccabeus, in the middle of the 2nd Century B.C.; but the latest archaeological finds, notably the coins, suggest that the first builder was probably his grandson, Alexander Jannai, also known in Hebrew as Jonathan the High Priest, some fifty years later.

It was king Herod, however, in the latter half of the 1st Century B.C., who turned it into a formidable fort, complete with stone casemate wall running round the top of the rock and enclosing the entire area; defence towers; barracks; arsenals; storehouses which Josephus later described as large enough to "store corn, wine and oil in abundance, as well as pulses and dates, such as would enable men to subsist for a long time"; large cisterns hewn out of the side of the cliff, linked by stone aqueduct to the Massada valley; a well-built palace on the western section of the rock; and an even more magnificent palace-villa built on three terraces scooped out of the cliff side just beneath the northern edge of the summit.

The Dead Sea.

This was the fortress which served the last band of Jewish fighters in their dramatic struggle against the Romans some 75 years after Herod's death. There is irony in the thought that these later zealots should so have profited from the works of Herod the renegade, whose power, including the power to strengthen the Massada fort, derived from Rome.

Herod carried out his building programme when he became king. But Massada had benefited him before he reached the throne. In the year 40 B.C., he lost the struggle for power with his Hasmonean rival, Mattathias Antigonus. Herod, grandson of an Idumaean convert to Judaism, had sought the support of the sovereign power, the Romans, to the disgust of the bulk of the Jews. Mattathias, popular with his people both because of his illustrious Jewish lineage — his great-grandfather was a nephew of Judas Maccabeus — and because he reflected their antipathy to Rome, sought the help of the Parthians. Together they scored an unexpected success and drove the Romans out of Jerusalem. Mattathias was crowned king. Herod promptly fled — to Massada, with his household and some of his followers. Leaving his younger brother there in charge of a garrison of 800, he set off to round up political support for his claims. He eventually made his way to Rome and secured his nomination as tributary king of Judea. Armed with this — and accompanied by two Roman legions — he returned in 37 B.C. and laid siege to Jerusalem. (During the siege he married Mariamne of the Royal Hasmonean house, hoping no doubt to garner some popularity among the Jews). After five months, Jerusalem fell. Mattathias, king for only three years, was put to death. Herod was enthroned in his stead. He was to reign for 33 years.

While he had been away, his small garrison of followers at Massada had been frequently attacked, but they had successfully held out against a more numerous foe. It was a tribute to their prowess. It was an even more impressive tribute to the natural defensive virtues of Massada. And who knew when he might not need such a protective retreat in the future? Now that he was king, he could make it a more formidable bastion by adding fortifications and installing supply facilities to withstand siege. And if by some mischance he should be forced to use it, he could build himself a palace befitting a man of his status. He set about these tasks without delay. It was during the period 37—30 B.C. that he built most of the structures on Massada whose ruins may be seen today.

The Roman besiegers of 72–73 A.D. also left signs of their presence. They include remains of their circumvallation, or siege wall, their camps at the foot of the rock, their earthworks, and the ramp for their battering ram and siege tower.

THE LAST STAND

In the year 70 A.D., when Jerusalem fell, after a four years' war of the Jews against the Romans, a band of Jewish patriots, led by Eleazar ben Yair, managed to escape. Determined to continue their battle for freedom, they made their way to Massada, which the Jews had captured from the Romans at the start of the revolt, in 66 A.D., and still held. With this stronghold as their base for raiding operations, they harried the Romans for two years. In 72 A.D., General Flavius Silva, a lieutenant of the Titus who conquered Jerusalem and destroyed the Temple, resolved to crush this outpost of resistance. He marched on Massada with his Tenth Legion, its auxiliary troops, and literally tens of thousands of prisoners of war to carry water, timber and provisions across the lengthy stretch of barren plateau. The Jews at the top of the rock prepared themselves for defence, making full use of the fortifications, and rationing the supplies in the storehouses and cisterns.

Silva's men tried to take the fortress but were beaten back. Bereft of swift victory, they were compelled to make elaborate arrangements for a lengthy siege. They established camps at the base of the rock — there are today the remains of at least eight. They built a three mile circumvallation round the fortress, guarded by troops to prevent flight or raiding sorties by the defenders. And on a rocky site near the western approach to Massada they constructed a solid ramp of beaten earth and large stones. On this they threw up a siege tower which dominated the rock. From its top, they hurled stones and fired arrows at the defenders. Under this covering fire, they moved a battering ram up the ramp, at the base of the tower, and directed it against the wall. They finally succeeded in effecting a breach. The defenders countered by rapidly building an inner wall at the point of attack. This wall consisted of a double stockade of wood filled with earth. The improvisation was ingenious. The blows of the battering ram, far from doing further damage, served to beat the earth into a more compact barrier.

But Flavius Silva was also not without ingenuity. Taking note of the defenders' new breastwork, he struck at its one weakness — the timber. Josephus writes: "Silva, finding that the battering with his machines did not produce the consequence he expected, ordered his soldiers to provide themselves with firebrands to destroy the works of the enemy. The new wall . . . immediately took fire, and the flames raged with the utmost violence. But the wind being at north it drove the fire with such rapidity on the Romans that they expected the almost instant destruction of their machines. But just at this juncture, the wind veered to the south, and beat so violently on the wall that the whole of it was in flames in a moment. The Romans, grateful for this providential stroke in their favour, returned to their camp full of spirits, and with a fixed determination to attack the enemy by break of day on the following morning; and, in the meantime, to place strong guards, that their opponents might not escape in the night."

But the Jewish leader, Eleazar ben Yair, had no thought of departing. His band

of Jewish patriots numbered 960, including women and children. The defensive wall was now consumed. There was no longer any security, and no hope of relief. Two alternatives alone were open: surrender or death. He resolved in his own mind "that a death of glory was preferable to a life of infamy, and that the most magnanimous resolution would be to disdain the idea of surviving the loss of their liberty."

He accordingly summoned his comrades and delivered what must assuredly be one of the most dramatic addresses in history — the more moving when one pictures the circumstances. It was recounted by the only survivors — two women and five children who failed to go through with Eleazar's plan, and hid themselves. It has been preserved for us in the writings of Josephus.

These were the words of Eleazar ben Yair on that fateful night on the top of Massada, uttered in the glow of the blazing wall:

"Will anyone who is not destitute of the common spirit of man wish to view the rising of another sun? Nay, would he wish it even if he might live in safety? Can anyone have so little regard to his country, so mean, so contracted a soul as not to regret that he has survived to behold this fatal day? Happy would it have been for us if we had all been sacrificed, rather than to have witnessed this sacrilegious destruction and to have beheld Jerusalem itself become a pile of ruins.

"While hope remained, however, our courage did not fail, and we despaired not of a happy change in our affairs. But as we have now no further reason to expect so auspicious a circumstance, and as we are urged by an invincible necessity to the step we ought now to take, it becomes us to have some regard to our wives, our children and ourselves; and in the plan of our proceeding we should be expeditious, while the means are yet in our power. All men are equally destined to death; and the same fate attends the coward as the brave. Can we think of submitting to the indignity of slavery? Can we behold our wives dishonoured and our children enslaved? Nature has not made this necessary; and if the evil arises, it must be from the force of cowardice and the fear of dying when we have it in our power. We had courage to abandon the Romans, to defy those who called themselves our masters, to reject their offered terms of quarter and pardon, and to refuse an indemnity when they besought us to accept it . . . While freedom is our own, and we are in possession of our swords, let us make a determined use of them to preserve our liberties. Let us die free men, gloriously surrounded by our wives and children. And let us be expeditious. Eternal renown shall be ours by snatching the prize from the hands of our enemies, and leaving them nothing to triumph over but the bodies of those who dared to be their own executioners."

Thus spake Eleazar. The response was unanimous. So long as there was hope,

they had fought. Now, with disaster inevitable, they would die by their own hand. They had little time. They moved without delay to the performance of their grim plan. "While they embraced their wives and children for the last time, they wept over and stabbed them in the same moment, taking comfort however that this work was not to be performed by their enemies ... There was not one man who was wanting in the necessary courage ...

"Those who had been the principal agents in this slaughter, smitten as they were with grief ... collected all their effects together and set them on fire. They then cast lots for the selection of ten men out of their number to destroy the rest. These being chosen, the devoted victims embraced the bodies of their deceased families and then, ranging themselves near them, resigned themselves to the hands of the executioners. When these ten men had discharged their disagreeable task, they again cast lots as to which of the ten should kill the other nine ... The nine devoted victims died with the same resolution as their brethren had done. And the surviving man, having surveyed the bodies and found that they were all dead, threw himself on his sword, among his companions ..."

At dawn next day, the Romans prepared themselves for the final assault. They were astonished at the lack of opposition when they showed themselves at the foot of their siege tower. Warily approaching the wall, they were still more surprised at encountering no defensive fire. When they entered, they heard no sound but the crackling of the flames. "On this", says Josephus, "they gave a loud shout, such as is customary when a battery is played off, in expectation of receiving an answer. This noise alarmed the two women in their place of retreat, who, immediately coming out, related the truth to the Romans as it really happened. The story however appeared so extraordinary that they could give no credit to it; but they exerted themselves in extinguishing the fire. And being employed in this service till they came to the palace, they there found the bodies of the deceased lying in heaps.

"Far, however, from exulting in the triumph of joy that might have been expected from enemies, they united to admire the steady virtue and dignity of mind with which the Jews had been inspired, and wondered at the generous contempt of death by which such numbers had been bound in one solemn compact."

It is perhaps not surprising that despite its antiquity, the richness of its relics, and the colourful description of its history and its original buildings by Josephus, Massada should so long have remained untouched by archaeological spade. For its forbidding approach to the besieger was equally dissuasive to the archaeologist. There were brief expeditions to this site in the last and the beginning of this century, but none was exhaustive. Most of the scholars were more concerned with the Roman remains and, set up camp at the foot of the rock, climbing to

the top only briefly to see the ruins on the plateau and to enjoy the view. The archaeologist Schulten, who worked for four weeks studying the Roman camps and siege walls in 1932, spent only two mornings on the summit. And he wrote: "One can envy the future explorer of the fortress his task, for it is varied and interesting, and the magnificent view is a reward in itself."

The first important study of the summit was undertaken only after the establishment of the State of Israel. It was sparked by the enthusiasm of a remarkable man, Shmaryahu Gutman, a farmer and member of a kibbutz, who has made a life-long hobby of Massada. It was he who discovered the "snake path" on the eastern escarpment, he who was the first to reach the northern palace, he who first explored the cisterns and traced the aqueduct to the wadi which received the floodwaters. He carried out an excavation in 1953 — with a volunteer team of fellow kibbutznicks — and it was largely as a result of his findings and his urgings that a more organised expedition by professional archaeologists was undertaken in 1955 and 1956. The 1955 team was headed by Professor Michael Avi-Yonah, Professor Nahman Avigad, Dr. Yohanan Aharoni and Shmaryahu Gutman. Aharoni and Gutman returned the following year to continue their investigations. They were unable to undertake a full scale excavation, but they carried out a survey of the area and examined the summit structures whose ruins were visible, both the Herodian structures and the remains of later buildings, including the 5th Century A.D. Byzantine church.

The most dramatic of the Herodian buildings which they examined was the palace built on three levels at the northern edge of the precipice. The living quarters proper were on the upper terrace, and there are remains of a large, rectangular, nine-roomed building and a magnificent semi-circular porch bounded by the side of the cliff. The floors are decorated with fine mosaics. The middle terrace, sixty feet below the summit, boasted a circular pavilion and a colonnade. Parts of two concentric masonry walls still stand. Forty feet below this terrace is the bottom tier of this extraordinary set of structures and is the best preserved. It holds the remains of a square building, with porticoed cloisters round a quadrangular open court, the fluted columns supported on attic bases and crowned with corinthian capitals. This building was decorated with wall paintings, most of which are intact.

The members of the 1955–56 expedition completed their brief seasons knowing that a thorough excavation of the entire site had yet to be made, and that it would require a large force equipped to tackle the tough topographic and logistic problems. This was undertaken by Professor Yigael Yadin in the autumn of 1963 when he launched a remarkable six months' dig. He received considerable aid from the Israel Defence Forces, and he took the unusual course of accepting volunteer "diggers" not only from Israel but from many countries

The Rock of Massada. (View from the south.)

overseas. He plans a second season of excavations in the winter of 1964/5. (As this edition goes to press, the work of reconstructing the ruins of Massada uncovered by the archaeologists is under way. It is being carried out by teams of experts from the Department of Landscaping and the Preservation of Historic Sites.) It was the Yadin expedition which determined that the hanging palace was in fact the palace-villa of Herod and not his main palace. It is the only spot on Massada which enjoys constant shelter from the searing desert winds and constant shade. Amid the debris in the rooms of this palace-villa Yadin found coins of the Jewish revolt, a letter in Aramaic, arrows, hundreds of silvered bronze scales of armour, and — gruesome evidence of the fate of the Jewish defenders who, as described by Josephus, had chosen death rather than surrender to the Romans — the remains of skeletons of a man, a woman and a youth. Dark brown plaits were still attached to the female scalp. Nearby were her sandals.

The large buildings just south of this villa were the store-rooms, whose walls and roofs had collapsed when the zealots set fire to the stores before their suicide. Jars were found, some containing remnants of food, which were made in Herod's time. They were also used by the zealots who had labelled their contents in Aramaic and Hebrew.

At the northwest corner of the storehouses, the expedition discovered a classic Roman bath-house of spacious proportions, complete with dressing room, hot room, tepid room and cold room. The floor of the hot room was raised, supported on pillars, and beneath it steam was introduced through square clay pipes.

The complex of Herodian buildings in the west is now seen, in the light of the Yadin excavations, to have been the main palace of Herod. It was a fine and well-planned royal residence, with throne room, reception halls, service quarters and workshops. Two excellent mosaic floors were uncovered.

Important discoveries awaited the archaeologists when they began excavating the fortress casemate wall. They revealed that when the patriots captured Massada in 66 A.D., they used the many chambers in the wall as living quarters. Here were found large quantities of domestic articles, such as baskets, clothing, shoes, sandals, cosmetic and cooking utensils, and numerous coins. Most moving were the small piles of ashes found in these zealots' dwelling rooms, the remains of their personal belongings which each family had carefully gathered in a corner and set on fire before submitting themselves to death.

Among these chambers within the casemate wall was one whose interior structure shows it to have been used for communal assembly. It is lined with rising tiers of mud and stone benches, and it is oriented towards Jerusalem. It is Yadin's interim hypothesis that this may have been the synagogue of the zealots. If he is right, this is the earliest known synagogue in existence and the only one belonging to the period of the Second Temple.

In the chamber close to the synagogue were fragments of scrolls of Genesis, Leviticus, Psalms and some apocryphal books. These were found with articles clearly belonging to the zealots, such as coins of the revolt. Here, then, at last, are Biblical documents definitely earlier than 73 A.D.! With them were found more than one hundred inscriptions on shards which show something of the way of life of the zealots. Several of them, like the record of payment of tithes, indicate a strict adherence to the commandments of the Torah.

There were two more scroll discoveries at the Massada excavations which are of considerable importance to scholars. One is a fragment whose text is identical with that of a scroll found at Qumran, site of the Dead Sea sect. The other proved to be fragments of a 1st Century B.C. Hebrew copy of Yehoshua ben-Sirah's apocryphal Book of Ecclesiasticus (which ben-Sirah had written in the previous century). It is the earliest copy of Ecclesiasticus in the world.

Among other discoveries of the Yadin expedition was an excellently preserved ritual bath (*mikveh*); many additional skeletons, found in a cave in the cliff face, believed to be those of zealots dumped there by the Romans; hundreds of Roman sling-shots, balls of stone the size of grapefruit, hurled by the Roman siege-engines and amassed by the defenders to fling back at their attackers; and some 2,200 coins. Among these were twenty silver shekels, the only ones ever found in an archaeological excavation. Three of them were dated the fifth year of the Jewish revolt — the year of the destruction of the Temple. Only six others are known to exist.

The dramatic location of Massada and the spectacular events that took place thereon give an added dimension to interest in the archaeological efforts to wrest the secrets from this fortress, the first to be captured from the Romans at the start of the great revolt and the last to hold out against them.

THE CAVES OF BAR KOCHBA

The wild primeval canyons which score the eastern escarpment of the Judean wilderness, near the shore of the Dead Sea between Massada and Ein Gedi, were the scene of the most adventurous archaeological excavations ever carried out in this part of the world. They were undertaken in the spring of 1960, and again in the following year, by four teams headed by archaeologists of Jerusalem's Hebrew University, the Israel Exploration Society and the Department of Antiquities. The team leaders were Dr. Yohanan Aharoni, Professors Nahman Avigad and Yigael Yadin, and Mr. Pesach Bar-Adon.

The focus of their search was the caves used as hide-outs by the followers of Bar Kochba who waged the second and final Jewish war against the Romans in 132—5 A.D. In the closing months of that bitter campaign, when freedom had been briefly won but was soon to be crushed, the remnants of the resistance fighters sought refuge for their families in these caves — which also served them as bases for guerrilla sorties against the enemy legions. The archaeologists considered that when Bar Kochba's men saw that the end was near, they may well have hidden their treasured documents in the floors or walls of the caves. The discovery of such Bar Kochba documents was the major aim of the expedition. If none was found, other relics might tell us more than we know of the final days of the last band of Jews to battle imperial Rome; for the history of this period is meagre in detail.

An event which prompted the organisation of this expedition was the dramatic discovery in 1947 of the Dead Sea Scrolls at a place called Khirbet Qumran, only a few miles to the north of the Judean caves it was now proposed to search. The first of these scrolls had been discovered by chance by a young bedouin goatherd who noticed a cave-opening in one of the rocks while going after a straying goat. Idly throwing a stone into the cave, he was surprised to hear the peculiar thud of stone on pottery. He crawled in to investigate. Within the cavern he found eight earthenware jars which contained bundles of inscribed parchment, some of them wrapped in linen. These were eventually brought to the bedouin market in Bethlehem and some were sold to an antique dealer, though neither bedouin nor dealer had the slightest inkling of their importance. The dealer showed them to Professor E.L. Sukenik, the Hebrew University archaeologist, and he was the first to detect, from a reading of the opening lines of the first parchment, that they were authentic documents from the period of the Second Temple. After much difficulty and danger — the Arab-Jewish war had just broken out — he managed to buy three of the seven scrolls discovered up to then: The War of the Sons of Light against the Sons of Darkness, the Thanksgiving Scroll, and a complete roll of the Biblical book of the prophet Isaiah. Under different but no less strange circumstances, his son, Professor Yigael Yadin, succeeded in 1954 in acquiring the other four scrolls from the Syrian Metropolitan, Mar Athanasius Samuel, of the Syrian Orthodox Monastery of St. Mark in Jerusalem, who had taken them to New York. These were The Manual of Discipline, The Habakkuk Commentary, The Genesis Apocryphon, and another complete scroll of Isaiah. All seven scrolls are now in Jerusalem, on permanent exhibition in the specially built Shrine of the Book.

The enormous world interest in these ancient documents — and the huge sums they could fetch — sent the bedouin scurrying among the Dead Sea cliffs in search of likely treasure caves. Some of them would even cross the border to

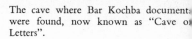

Bundle of documents as they were found in the Caves of Bar Kochba.

investigate the more accessible caves within the territory of Israel. Early in 1952 they found a few documents which appeared to relate to Bar Kochba. Two small scale Israeli surveys were then undertaken by Dr. Aharoni, but he was favoured with no major finds. He reported that some of the caves showed signs of recent ferreting by bedouin, but that searches of the more inaccessible spots might prove rewarding. It was evident that such searches, to be thorough, would involve the mounting of a full scale expedition. Appropriate equipment would be required to enter and excavate those caves which, in Bar Kochba's time, must have been difficult for the Roman legionaries to get to, and which, in our own time, were beyond the reach of bedouin. This was the expedition which went on its exploration of the Dead Sea cliffs in 1960. The scale of its operations was made possible only by the cooperation of the Israel Defence Forces.

The caves selected for investigation have their openings in the sheer walls of canyons, most of them inaccessible today on foot except by experienced rock-climbers. Even in ancient days the approach must have been excessively difficult — and for that reason chosen by the rebels; but it was at least possible, no doubt across narrow goat tracks which have since been obliterated or eroded down to perilous ledges. Some of the caves in the steep cliff-side are 150 feet below the lip of the summit and 750 feet above the floor of the gorge. Preliminary reconnaissance was carried out by helicopter. Where traces were visible of an old trail leading to the mouth of a cave, but where the track itself was now impassable, the cave was marked down for exploration.

The opening days of the archaeological expediton were spent in widening some of the tracks, rendering others usable by putting up rope rails, and preparing rope ladders which were slung over the side of the cliff. Much of this was performed by army volunteers who did their work dangling at the end of ropes picketed to stakes on the plateau above. The daily approach to the caves was a hazardous venture for the archaeologists. Once inside they faced the further danger of rock-falls and collapsing roofs, as well as the discomforts of working in a foetid atmosphere. Some caves contained additional rock chambers which could be reached only through constricted tunnels negotiable by crawling on all fours and at times by wriggling one's body through — properly roped so that one could be withdrawn if the tunnel terminated in a dead end. Work within was possible only for short periods at a time; and then the lungs cried out for fresh air. Members of the expedition agreed, however, that it had been worth while. Some of the finds were spectacular and revolutionary, and all four teams found relics of considerable historic interest. It was promptly resolved to repeat the performance. This took place in the spring of 1961 when further impressive discoveries were registered. Plans are now being considered to build access paths to the caves where the most important finds were made.

Professor Avigad concentrated on what is now known as the "Cave of the Pool" in Nahal David, just north of Ein Gedi, and he found remains from the Chalcolithic, Israelite and Roman periods. Most important was the water pool near the cave entrance, partly hewn out of the rock and partly built up, faced with high quality plaster. It was fed by rainwater which entered the pool from above through a vertical gully, part of which is preserved. The structure reflects imagination in its conception and daring in its execution. It dates to the period of Bar Kochba. Avigad believes that it was the work of Jewish notables of Ein Gedi, local leaders under Bar Kochba in the revolt against the Romans, who had made emergency provision for refuge against siege. When the prospect became hopeless, they retired to this hide-out. The excavations showed that they must have been pursued right up to the cave. An iron arrow-head was found lodged in the roof near the entrance, having been fired from the outside.

Dr. Aharoni's area of investigation was Nahal Seelim, one of the biggest canyons in the Judean desert which drains into the Dead Sea about 2½ miles north of Massada, and its western extension which is called Nahal Hardof. He, too, found remains of structures as well as ancient relics belonging to the Chalcolithic, Israelite and Bar-Kochba periods. Aharoni did not confine his study to caves alone. He reconnoitred the whole valley and discovered remains of fortresses belonging both to the Israelite and to the Roman periods. Examining several caves, each more difficult to reach than the other, he found in one a bronze coin from the second year of Bar Kochba, and in another an arsenal of arrows. His chief prize, discovered in a third cave, was fragments of parchment and papyri, unearthed from a small pit near the entrance together with objects and coins. More fragments of papyri were found in the same cave beneath a vulture's nest. The coins date to one hundred years *after* the Bar Kochba revolt. The written material includes portions of the phylactery prayers in minute Hebrew writing; a parchment containing part of the Hebrew text of Chapter 13 of Exodus; another piece of parchment with another part of the same chapter of Exodus; the corner of a leather scroll containing Hebrew letters; and several fragments of papyri some with Hebrew and others with Greek writing.

His survey and excavations led Aharoni to the conclusion that in the final stage of the revolt, a group of Bar Kochba's soldiers found refuge in the caves of the Seelim and Hardof canyons, just as others went to other valleys in the region. He discovered a cistern in one of the caves similar to that in the "Cave of the Pool" near Ein Gedi, indicating that here, too, the hiding place had been prepared beforehand. The fragmentary nature and damaged condition of the portions of scrolls and manuscripts, and of such relics as leather phylactery strips, suggest that the Bar Kochba fighters had assuredly hidden their holy texts and religious articles in the caves, and that these had probably been removed one hundred years

Original wicker basket as found during excavations, containing Roman ritual vessels of bronze.

The hoard of Chalcolithic copper objects as found in cave.

5000-year old ornamental copper objects from the unique Chalcolithic hoard found during excavations of Caves of Bar Kochba.

Two faces of bronze coin struck by Bar Kochba.

later, about the time indicated by the later coins. These finds, and the absence of any signs of Roman siege similar to those at the canyons further north, suggest that the group who held out in Nahal Seelim were not caught by the enemy.

The area examined by Bar-Adon covered the southern bank of Nahal Hever and the canyons of Holed, Asahel and Mishmar. They lie to the north of Nahal Seelim and southwest of Ein Gedi. Relics belonging to the Bar Kochba period were found in an interesting cave in Nahal Mishmar, now called the "Scout's Cave", which was inhabited as far back as the Chalcolithic period. There were two fragments of papyri, one with Greek and one with Hebrew writing; numerous potsherds of lamps, jars, jugs and other vessels; and pieces of leather, woven fabric, sacking, matting and remnants of baskets, all dating to the 1st and 2nd Centuries A.D. Artefacts and remnants of leather and textiles were also found in the Chalcolithic strata.

Bar-Adon's most astonishing discovery, however, occurred in the following year in a cave in Nahal Hever. This was a cache of some 420 objects belonging to the 4th millennium B.C., the largest archaeological treasure of the Chalcolithic period ever unearthed. The objects were wrapped in a mat and had been secreted in the wall of the cave. They consisted of copper tools, mace-heads, sceptres, crowns, staves and standards of great beauty and technical artistry; and well fashioned and decoratively worked hippopotamus ivories. Some of them resemble the Chalcolithic relics found near Beersheba in the subterranean settlement excavated by the French archaeologist Jean Perrot some years before. Bar-Adon believes that these objects belonged to some temple or palace and were buried in this cave in time of war, the owners no doubt hoping to return. They never did, and the treasure was so well hidden that five thousand years were to elapse before its discovery.

The team that was most fortunate in the discovery of Bar Kochba documents was the one headed by Yadin. His area of exploration covered the southern cliffs of Nahal Arugot, the northern cliffs of Nahal Hever, and the eastern cliffs linking the two canyons. The most exciting yields came from a large cave in Nahal Hever, southwest of Ein Gedi, and it is therefore now known as the "Cave of Letters".

A happy augury at the start of the exploration was the discovery of a Bar Kochba bronze coin just outside the cave entrance. One side of the coin bore the design of a palm tree and the inscription "Shimon" — Bar Kochba's first name. The other side showed a cluster of grapes and the Hebrew inscription "Leherut Yerushalayim" — "For the freedom of Jerusalem". The first finds inside the cave were Roman bronze ritual vessels in a wicker basket. The reliefs of ornamental images on some of the vessels had been deliberately defaced by scratching. This suggests that the vessels were booty taken from a Roman unit by Bar Kochba's soldiers.

More important, however, were the manuscripts. One was a parchment fragment from the Biblical Book of Psalms, containing parts of Psalms 15 and 16 in Hebrew. The rest were Bar Kochba letters, in which he is referred to as "Shimon Bar Kosiba" — the name by which he is known in Rabbinic literature. The more familiar "Bar Kochba", which is Hebrew for "Son of a Star", was the name given him by his admirers. The discovery of these letters confirms, for the first time, that his name was in fact Bar Kosiba.

The letters were excavated from a small cavity in a corner of one of the chambers in this large cave, together with several objects, such as a knife, mirror and a water skin made of animal hide. Inside the skin was a bundle of papyri wrapped in a kerchief knotted at the ends. Between the papyri were four thin slats of wood covered by writing. When removed, the slats were found to be parts of a single "sheet" of wood which had been "folded" into four and was inscribed with two columns of Aramaic writing. It was a letter which opened with the words: "Shimon Bar Kosiba, the Prince over Israel, to Yehonatan and Masabala, peace." Of the fifteen letters found in this bundle, this was the only one which records the full title of Bar Kochba.

It is Yadin's view that the letters were brought to this cave by Yehonatan or Masabala when they took refuge there. The water skin in which the documents were hidden probably belonged to the wife of one of them — hence the knife and the mirror. The general style of the letters indicates that they were written in the final stage of the war — in the year 134 or 135 A.D. The early ones were in Greek and Aramaic and the later ones in Hebrew. It was probably by command of Bar Kochba that Hebrew was later made compulsory for official correspondence.

Who were Yehonatan and Masabala? This was to remain a mystery until the following year when a further exploration was undertaken. It was then found that these two men were the military and civil heads of Ein Gedi serving under Bar Kochba. The letter written on wood contained orders to them from their commander.

In 1961, further searches of the "Cave of Letters" yielded an amazing find of documents, many of them containing names, titles and dates — the very information, most rare, which makes it possible to fix with absolute certainty the period of an archaeological stratum. One of the documents begins: "On 28th of Marheshvan (a Jewish month) year three of Shimon ben Kosiba Prince of Israel . . ." This is a deed leasing land. The lessor is "Yehonatan . . . administrator of Shimon ben Kosiba Prince of Israel, in Ein Gedi". The subject was state lands which were leased to residents through the heads of administrative centres, acting on behalf of Bar Kochba.

The prize package was a bundle of 36 papyrus documents which turned out to be

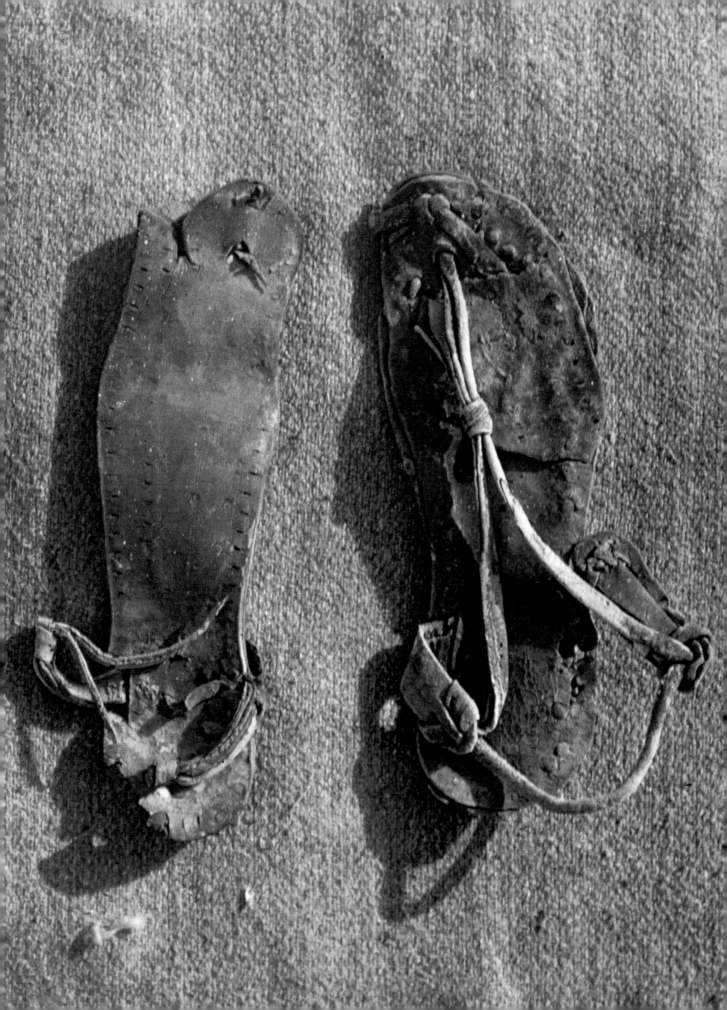

the complete family archive belonging to a certain lady named Babata. Some of the documents were in Hebrew, others in Aramaic, Greek and Nabatean. Through them, the scholars were able to recapitulate the life of Babata — clearly the well-organised daughter of a rich and distinguished family — from her youth up to the time of Bar Kochba's great revolt; and through her life it was possible to trace the prevailing pattern of contemporary society in Judea and the Dead Sea area. This family archive tells us much of the legal patterns, linguistic forms and social make-up of the times, and fills several gaps in our knowledge of the history of this period — not only in Palestine. For example, some of the legal deeds use three systems of dating: the year is given by reference to the Consul of the year in Rome; to the Roman emperor at the time — e.g "the third year of Hadrian", who started his reign in 117 A.D.; and by reference to the year of "Provincia Arabia" — the Roman province established by Trajan in 106 A.D. in place of the Nabatean vassal kingdom in Palestine; the "fifteenth year of Provincia Arabia" would therefore be 121 A.D. The documents thus offer a complete synchronisation of the three systems. They also refer to several Roman Consuls whose names are missing from the Roman sources, and the list can now be completed for the first time.

Here are some examples of how the documents open windows to the patterns of living of those times, the relations between the governors and the governed, the legal system, trade transactions, the forms of agriculture, the monetary system and property rights. One of the documents is a "gift deed" whereby Babata's father assigns to his wife all his property as a life gift. It states that he is a resident of the village of Mahoza, in the district of Zoar, at the southern tip of the Dead Sea. It lists his possessions in detail, defining the boundaries of his land, mostly under date plantation, and sets forth the water rights accompanying each tract, indicative of an advanced farming organisation. Another document shows that five years before the revolt, Babata journeyed with her husband to the head-quarters of the Roman cavalry unit in Rabbat Moab to declare her property for a land census taken that year by the governor of Provincia Arabia. Expected yields of dates were listed according to their category and quality. One transaction recorded in another document stipulates that the lessee of part of Babata's lands must pay her 42 talents of dates of superior quality and a specified quantity of inferior dates, the amounts to be weighed in her house on Mahoza scales. The balance is to be kept by the lessee "for my labour and expenses" — an early form of share-cropping.

A document belonging to the year 124 A.D. relates to a loan taken by Babata's husband, Yehuda, a year before their marriage and his move to Mahoza, when he was still living in Ein Gedi. It records that Yehuda has borrowed 60 Tyrian silver dinars from Valens, centurion of the First Thracian Cohort of a thousand infantry.

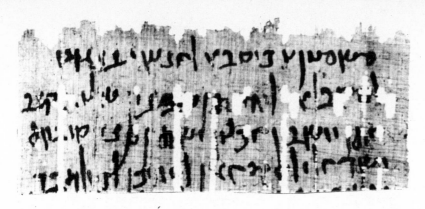

A letter from Shimon Bar Kosiba (Bar Kochba) to the commander in Ein Gedi of the Jewish revolt against the Romans. Written on papyrus in Hebrew.

He pledges to repay the loan plus one per cent monthly interest in eight months. As security he offers his father's compound, whose boundaries are defined. This document shows that eight years before the Bar Kochba revolt a company of one hundred Thracian auxiliaries was stationed at Ein Gedi. Yadin has suggested that with the outbreak of the Bar Kochba revolt, the Jews of Ein Gedi apparently fought this Roman unit, and the cult objects found in the 1960 expedition with their ritual decorations defaced may conceivably have belonged to them. Incidentally the definition of the boundaries of the compound pledged by Yehuda against his loan mentions "north — the road and the fort". This fort may well be the burnt-out citadel recently discovered by archaeologists at Ein Gedi.

How did these documents — and Babata — reach the cave? One of them reveals that she was a distant relative of the Yehonatan who, together with Masabala, led the Jewish contingent of Ein Gedi during the revolt. When they fled to the caves towards the end of the fighting, she must have been in the group, carrying her precious archive with her.

In addition to documents, Yadin and his team also found unique basket work and textiles which include the oldest garment designed like a Roman toga ever discovered. Its shape and style were known from writings and illustrations. But nothing so ancient has ever come to light, not even in Italy where they were plentiful, for all have rotted with time. Only in the dry "air-conditioned" atmosphere of the Dead Sea caves have they been preserved, and can now be handled and examined. One curious result is that terms relating to such garments in the Talmud, which had not been quite understood before, now become clear. A study of the materials, the weave, the embroidery and the dyes of this unique collection of ancient textiles, soon to be published by Yadin, will add considerably to our knowledge of the crafts, skills, habits and customs of those early days.

EIN GEDI

Ten miles north of Massada, also close to the Dead Sea shore, is the small emerald-green settlement of Ein Gedi. This beauty spot is one of nature's freaks. For while it lies at the edge of the bleak Wilderness of Judea and only a few hundred yards from the Sea of Salt, it is rich with lush vegetation, nourished the year round by sweet-water springs and natural water-falls. Through the foliage come sounds of water cascading over the rocks — joyous music in these hot low-altitude surroundings — and pouring into pools which are fresh and icy at all times.

Hebrew inscription on stone seal found at Ein Gedi, 7th Century B.C.

Ein Gedi is Hebrew for "Fountain of the Kid". It was one of the ancient cities of Judah, and finds frequent mention in the Bible. It was here that David sought shelter from one of the periodic moods of anger of king Saul. When Saul was told "Behold, David is in the wilderness of En-gedi", he went after him with three thousand troops "to seek David and his men upon the rocks of the wild goats" (I Samuel XXIV). But David, forewarned, remained hidden. Emerging while Saul was resting, he came close enough to "cut off the skirt of Saul's robe privily", showing that he could have slain the king had he so wished. This gesture moved the contrite Saul to banish his misgivings about David's loyalty. "And he said to David, Thou art more righteous than I: for thou hast rewarded me good, whereas I have rewarded thee evil."

Solomon in Song of Songs sang "My beloved is unto me as a cluster of camphor in the vineyards of En-gedi", a clear indication that this was a flourishing spot three thousand years ago. In the centuries that followed, it experienced the successive pattern of destruction and reconstruction common to those uncertain times. It was during one of its periods of desolation that the Roman historian Pliny wrote his lament, one thousand years after Solomon: "Its groves of palm trees are now like Jerusalem, a heap of ashes".

But not for long. From the archaeological excavations in the caves of the Judean Wilderness, only a few miles from Ein Gedi, we know that in the beginning of the 2nd Century A.D., it supported a lively Jewish settlement.

More specific details of the material history of Ein Gedi in ancient times have recently become known through excavations carried out on the spot by a team of Israeli archaeologists headed by Professor Benjamin Mazar. The earliest finds were Chalcolithic, and among the remains of this period was a large temple built on the hill above the main Ein Gedi spring. It consisted of an enclosure with an altar in the centre, and three buildings, one of them well preserved, which clearly served as a hall of worship. Of post-Solomonic settlement, they found relics from the days of king Josiah of Judah and his successors, in addition to strata belonging to the Persian, Hellenistic, Hasmonean and Roman periods. Ein Gedi was one of the few places in the country where the balsam tree flourished, and during the time of the Israelite kings the local industry was the manufacture of precious perfume from this tree. The archaeologists found many of the special vessels and bone and metal tools used in the preparation of the perfume, as well as graduated weights inscribed with the measure.

Only a few miles south of Qumran, Ein Gedi may well have been a familiar place to the members of the ancient Jewish sect who secreted their "Dead Sea Scrolls" in nearby caves.

AVDAT

On the spur of a low dun-coloured hill of rugged limestone, in the heart of the Negev desert, stand the eloquent remains of an ancient city. On this site, a skilled and industrious people once flourished, combining agriculture with commerce. They engaged in trade, establishing settlements like this to guard their caravan routes, and they grew their own food, conceiving ingenious devices to trap water to nourish the soil which they had reclaimed from the desert. They converted this spot into a garden city in the midst of the forbidding wilderness of Zin. The people were the Nabateans, and this was their city of Avdat.

The Nabateans were a tribal people who gradually moved northwards from Arabia and began to settle in Transjordan and the Negev at the end of the 4th and beginning of the 3rd Century B.C. Not very long before the area fell under the domination of the Romans, they had carved out for themselves an extensive kingdom with their capital at Petra, east of the Jordan. Their period of real glory, however, was brief, covering the hundred or so years from the middle of the 1st Century B.C. to the middle of the 1st Century A.D., but the relics they left of that period show them to have excelled as traders, farmers, engineers, architects and artists. As the archaeologist Dr. Nelson Glueck observes, "They may be accounted one of the most remarkable peoples of history. Sprung swiftly out of the desert of Arabia to a position of great power and affluence, they were thrust back by the Romans even more swiftly into the limbo whence they came . . . The phenomenon of their appearance and disappearance between the first centuries B.C. and A.D. may be likened to the brilliance of a meteor flashing briefly across the skies to blazing extinction."

Archaeological evidence now shows Avdat to have been established by the Nabateans in the 3rd Century B.C. and to have lasted about one thousand years, long after the founding nation had vanished. Apart from Nabatean remains found on the site, there are 3rd Century A.D. burial chambers cut in the hillsides and buildings from the same and later periods on top of the hill, notably additions to a fine Nabatean terrace offering a commanding view of the entire region. Nearby are 6th and 7th Century Byzantine structures, including two churches and a monastery, part of the city wall and the remains of an impressive fortress. There are also ruined Byzantine dwellings in front of the earlier caves on the hill-slopes.

Avdat lies on the new arterial road through the Negev, 40 miles south of Beersheba and 105 miles north of Elath. (The nearest village to Avdat is Sde Boker, the desert settlement retreat of ex-Prime Minister David Ben Gurion, a fifteen minutes drive to the north.) A few miles to the south lies the stark and majestic

crater, Makhtesh Ramon. A rubbled declivity between the rocks behind Avdat leads to an icy pool, called Ein Avdat, fed by flood waters which flow southwards along an intricate network of channels fashioned by nature.

To consolidate their rule in the Negev, the Nabateans sought to protect their trade by establishing settlements at key points along their caravan routes. Spices, textiles and precious gems were brought from Southern Arabia and India to Petra and Elath, and from there the Nabateans carried them across the Negev to the Mediterranean outlets at Gaza and Rafah. The routes to the Mediterranean from Petra and Elath met in the vicinity of Avdat. This was their primary reason for establishing a settlement here. Agricultural prospects favoured their choice.

The land round Avdat was the first extensive area north of the Rimon Crater in which cultivation seemed at all possible. In their farming, the Nabateans applied the techniques of desert agriculture which their predecessors, the Judeans, had devised. They also introduced their own improvements. The principal problem then, as now, was water. Their method was to conserve rain water by a system of dams and cisterns and to cut channels along which they could direct runoff waters from the hills. They were thus able to hoard sufficient water to irrigate the fields of the small Nabatean farms which dotted the valley round the hill-city of Avdat. A farm restoration programme was started in 1959 by Professor Michael Even-Ari, Professor of Botany at the Hebrew University, and a team of Israeli botanists and agrarian experts. They are reconstructing on the fields round Avdat the farming pattern followed by the Nabateans, growing the same crops by the same methods and using the same water conservation and irrigation techniques used in ages past.

Strategically, Avdat, on high ground, commanded the plains of the southeast, south and west, the direction of the caravan trails. This gave them warning of raids, and if hard-pressed they could fortify themselves in their hill-top stronghold.

Avdat takes its name from one of the Nabatean kings called Obodas (Abdat) — he is believed to have been Obodas II — who died towards the end of the 1st Century B.C. and, according to tradition, was buried here. Obodas II, a contemporary of king Herod the Great, was the father of the most powerful of the Nabatean kings, Aretas IV, who reigned from 9 B.C. to 40 A.D. Incidentally, it was a daughter of Aretas who became the wife, later divorced, of king Herod's most able son, Herod Antipas, the Tetrarch of Galilee who built Tiberias.

Nabatean rule came to an end in the year 106 A.D. with the annexation of their kingdom by the Roman emperor Trajan, though a Nabatean inscription found and deciphered by Avraham Negev shows that Avdat continued in existence for

at least another twenty years. Shortly thereafter, the Romans built their great road linking Elath with Damascus which by-passed Avdat and diverted trade from this region. The city fell into decline. Not until the middle of the 3rd Century did it begin to recover. The Roman emperor Diocletian, who ruled from 284 to 305 A.D., renewed the defences of the Roman border, constructing a series of forts along the routes linking the Arabah Valley with the northern Negev. Avdat was one of the sites chosen for such a fort. The Roman camp northeast of the city is believed to belong to this period. And from inscriptions, coins and pottery, archaeologists date the watchtower and colonnaded terrace as having been constructed at this time.

From now on, Avdat began to regain its former prosperity, reaching its most flourishing period in the 6th Century. It was during this Byzantine period that the fortress at the top of the hill was built to protect the settled population from attacks by nomadic bedouin tribes. To this period, too, belongs the construction of the two churches, the monastery, the baptistry, the additions to the hill-top terrace, the houses and city wall in the upper part of the city and the cutting of new dwelling caves in the lower slopes.

The second decline of Avdat started with the Moslem conquest of the Negev in 634 A.D., though it apparently fell without resistance. The new rulers, close to the nomadic ways, were less concerned than their predecessors with protecting the interests of cities along their caravan routes. Avdat to them was simply the place which boasted a bath-house at the foot of the hill, and this their travellers used. In the 10th Century, the site was finally abandoned.

It remained forgotten until 1871 when the British traveller Palmer came across its ruins. A small-scale archaeological excavation was undertaken by the Dunscombe Colt expedition in 1935. Renewed interest in this ancient city followed the establishment of the nearby settlement of Sde Boker in 1949 by a group of young pioneer men and women who had served in the Negev during Israel's War of Independence. Its recent clearance and restoration were carried out under the guidance of the archaeologists Professor Michael Avi-Yonah and Dr. Avraham Negev of the Hebrew University of Jerusalem.

A short access road off the main highway brings you to the first signs of ancient habitation at the foot of the hill upon which Avdat was built. These are caves cut in tiers in the sloping rock and used as tombs and they belong to the Byzantine period. At times during this period, houses were constructed in front of the caves. None is now complete, but one has been reconstructed, consisting of two large courts linked by several passages in which the remains of a drainage system are to be seen. The passages gave on to living rooms, roofed in a manner characteristic of construction in a treeless region. In place of wooden beams, the rooms

Bronze leopard found in Nabatean ruins at Avdat, 1st Century A.D.

were vaulted by three parallel stone arches which held a layer of flat stones. Behind this house is a cave used as a dwelling, with the addition of a closing wall near the entrance. One room had been preserved as a storage chamber. One room served as a praying chapel, its roof decorated with two crosses in relief adorned by a sculptured human figure and heads of animals. The wall of another room bears primitive drawings of Saints and inscriptions invoking heaven's protection.

From here a winding path takes you to the top of the hill, past the remains of the Byzantine wall. Further up, you reach the 20 foot high terrace wall which supported a portico. Behind it were found fifteen casemates, hollow chambers built between double walls. To the right of the path is part of a winding staircase, found in situ, which belongs to the beginning of the 1st Century A.D. It was built during the reign of Aretas IV to give access to a Nabatean temple. Nearby is the terrace, also built in the 1st Century, probably as an open esplanade. The bases of a row of columns of a later period suggest that it was turned into a covered area, the roof supported by a colonnade. At its northern end are four pillars on which rested a Byzantine balcony. During the Byzantine period the terrace was reached by the stairway at the left, which is in use today.

From here one gains entry to a narrow street at the northern end of which is a stone bench with curved head-rest. It probably stood near an opening which commanded a view of the northern approaches. Along this street is the baptistry, built in the 6th Century as a three-walled room with two columns standing in front of an open entrance. The baptismal font is in the form of a cross, faced with marble. Near it is a small font for babies. Behind the main font is a wall of the apse; to the left is a pillar with a niche which was probably used as a depository of ritual objects.

Behind the street are the ruins of the 6th Century North Church with two rows of columns dividing it into nave and aisles. Some of the fine stones used in its construction were taken from the ruins of the Nabatean temple. The altar, which stood in front of a semi-circular apse, was separated from the rest of the church by a raised chancel-screen, part of which still stands. In the apse is the stone seat of the bishop and behind it a semi-circular stone bench for the clergy. The stone at the left is the base of the preaching platform.

Outside this church are the ruins of a 6th Century monastery adjoining another church, the later of the two. This is the South Church, whose architectural plan is similar to that of the northern basilica. On the walls of the two small niches on either side of the central apse are the remains of frescoes representing holy figures. This church has several 7th Century tombstones, one of them recording the burial of the head of the monastery in the year 618 A.D. The South Church is now also known as the Church of St. Theodorus.

South of this complex of buildings is a rectangular Byzantine fortress with towers at each corner and in the middle of each wall. Above the northern entrance is a stone bearing a cross with symbolic letters between the arms of the cross. The fortress encompassed a large space free of buildings — used probably as a refuge for the people during bedouin raids. A deep cistern in the centre was fed by a conduit leading from the outside. About 150 yards to the east of the fortress the archaeologists made a unique find — a Nabatean potter's workshop, complete with kiln and the base of a potter's wheel. The floor was strewn with excellent examples of Nabatean pottery. To the·south of the citadel are the remains of a wine press. Further south are the ruins of houses. At the bottom of the southern slope stands an isolated Byzantine dwelling overlooking the valley.

At the foot of the hill is an ancient bath-house and well. The well is still in use. A Greek inscription near the entrance shows that it dates from the Byzantine period. The floors of the two "hot rooms" of the bath-house rest on brick pillars. The hollow space below the pillars carried the heat from outside ovens, warming the floors. The heat was also passed upwards in vertical pipes lining the walls. One of the bathrooms has a cylindrical vault. The other is domed and has brick bath-tubs in three of its niches.

A museum on the spot contains statuettes, implements, pottery vessels, potsherds and Greek and Nabatean inscriptions discovered during the clearance of the site.

SHIVTA

Shivta, also a Nabatean-Byzantine city, founded somewhat later than its sister city Avdat, is situated in the northwestern Negev. It, too, has recently been restored under the direction of Professor Avi-Yonah, and you can now walk through the narrow streets of the city and absorb the very flavour of antiquity. You can see houses, some still standing to the second storey, made of stone which was soft when freshly quarried but which hardened when exposed to sun and wind. You can peep through windows, small and narrow to provide ventilation without inviting the burning rays, and conjure the design for living of families who dwelt here so many centuries ago. You can gauge their standards of architecture from the remains of fine churches. Their techniques of water conservation may be seen in the built-in pottery pipes which channeled the water from the flat rooftops to cisterns below the dwelling rooms, and in the well-preserved public reservoirs in the main square.

Shivta is now easily reached by a newly paved road which runs off the main Beersheba-Nitzana highway. It lies at the end of a low ridge of parchment-coloured hills which separate the valleys of Zeitan and Korha. It is some 28 miles southwest of Beersheba and 12 miles east of the Sinai border.

Unlike any other Nabatean city, the site of Shivta has no special strategic value. It commanded no important highway and no ancient trading route. Nor was it fortified. The primary reason for its settlement is believed to have been the suitability of its land for cultivation under the Nabatean system of irrigation. And the agricultural produce apparently went to feed the nearby important caravan station of Nitzana which stood astride the main trail linking Egypt and the Sinai peninsula with Rafah and Gaza.

The name (in Greek, Subeita) stems from the original Nabatean meaning of "small tribe". This, together with its distance from a main route and the absence of a fortified wall, suggests that it was established by a small Nabatean group or tribe as a farm village. Its origin and the date of its foundation — 2nd or 1st Century B.C. — were easily determined from the two special Nabatean "trade-marks" which underwent slight variations from century to century throughout their existence: their water-conservation system and their pottery. Nabatean potsherds are unmistakeable. They are among the most beautiful products of the ancient potter's craft, thin and delicate, with decorations of plant designs on a red or brown background.

As with Avdat, Shivta's progress was halted with the Roman conquest of the Nabateans in 106 A.D. The Romans indeed maintained it as a useful supply centre for their garrisons in the northern Negev. But they did little to develop it. Only with the rise of Byzantine rule in the 4th Century did Shivta again begin to flourish, and again, as with Avdat, it began to decline with the Moslem conquest of the region in 634 A.D.

The first mention of Shivta in ancient literary documents occurs in a 5th Century A.D., tragi-comic tale of a young pilgrim. St. Nilus, a distinguished Prefect of Constantine who spent years of his life in Sinai, recounts the story of his pupil Theodulos who was kidnapped while on a pilgrimage to Sinai by a pagan bedouin band. They decided to offer him as a sacrifice to the Morning Star. Fortunately for the young man, his captors overslept. By first light, the Morning Star had disappeared. The bedouin took this as a sign that young Theodulos had been rejected by the Star as an unacceptable offering. He was spared. Their next best course was to take him to the slave-market at Shivta where the Saracenic bedouin brought their captives for sale. Theodulos was sold; but when his plight reached the ears of the Christian authorities in Halutza, the district centre at the time and some 15 miles north of Shivta, they redeemed him.

Ornamental capital found in ruins of Shivta.

So all ended well. The story, related to Nilus, was recorded by him in his Narrations.

Shivta is also mentioned several times in the 6th and 7th Century A.D. papyri found at Nitzana. Cufic inscriptions show the town to have been inhabited until the 12th Century. Arab glazed sherds were also found in the vicinity of Shivta dating possibly to the 13th or 14th Century. From then on the city stood deserted, forgotten and undisturbed until 1839 when it was discovered by Edward Robinson, the American theologian and "father" of biblical topography. It was visited in 1914 by a British survey expedition whose ostensible interest was archaeology but who were fully aware of the importance of the Negev in any subsequent military action against the Turks. Three members of this expedition were later to achieve considerable fame — Lawrence, Woolley and Newcombe. In 1916, a German survey team visited Shivta and were the first to take aerial photographs of the site. In 1935–37 an Anglo-American excavation was carried out under the direction of the archaeologist Harris Dunscombe Colt.

The oldest part of Shivta is its southern quarter, which is clearly pre-Christian. It contained two public reservoirs which were fed by water channels lining the streets. In Christian times, the site chosen for the principal church, now called the South Church, was close to these reservoirs, no doubt because this was the most frequented part of the quarter. A study of its construction plan reveals the scrupulous care taken to avoid interference with streets and channels.

Still standing are the numerous houses, built of stone, some with carved doorposts and ornamented window-frames. They consisted of two or three large rooms and several smaller cubicles, mostly built round a courtyard. The roofs were flat, to serve as catchments for rain water, and each house had one or two cisterns. In the old quarter, the cisterns were sunk in the centre of the courtyard and fed by open channels. Later, as in the northern quarter, improvements were introduced. Cisterns were now installed beneath the rooms and water flowed from the roof through pottery pipes built into walls during the construction of the house.

Stern discipline seems to have been enforced on the inhabitants to ensure water conservation. It is clear that building regulations demanded provision for a catchment and cistern in every structure. Every citizen had also to help maintain the public water system. A number of ostraca discovered in Shivta were receipts for such services. One of them reads: "To Flavius Gormos son of Zachariah: You have completed one corvee (turn of duty) for the reservoir. Written on the 25th Dios in the 9th Indiction". Flavius had done his stint on reservoir-cleaning!

Evidence of some town planning exists in the northern part of the town.

There is a wide paved square near the North Church, flanked by shops, a wine-press and baking ovens. The market place and trading centre were probably situated here.

Just outside the town, about five hundred yards to the northeast, are the terraced fields enclosed by stone hedges and served by an irrigation system of channels, dykes and sluice-gates first devised by Nabateans and extended by the Byzantines. Here, too, as at Avdat, Professor Even-Ari carried out an agricultural restoration programme.

Entering Shivta from the southwest, you reach a square which contains the two large reservoirs. These are cut out of the rock and lined with a covering of small stones embedded in hydraulic cement to prevent seepage.

Beyond the reservoirs is the 5th Century South Church with its ante-room (narthex) leading to a long hall with two rows of columns dividing it into nave and aisles. The hall ends in three semi-circular apses. In front of the central apse stood an altar on a raised platform which was originally enclosed by a chancel screen.

Entry to the adjoining baptistry was through the narthex. It contains a well-preserved monolithic font in the shape of a cross. Steps into the font are cut in the eastern and western arms of the cross.

Close to it is the mosque built some four hundred years later. Its mihrab — the niche which indicates the direction of Mecca — impinges slightly on the baptistry without, however, disturbing its internal arrangements.

Proceeding northwards, you pass the Centre Church and tower and reach the paved square near the North Church. Beyond the eastern side of the square is a wine-press, with a paved platform on which the grapes were crushed, the juice flowing through a channel to a round vat cut in the floor of a lower room.

The North Church, the latest of the three, consists of a court or atrium which was originally surrounded by colonnades. Like the South Church, it ends in three apses and is divided into nave and aisles by two rows each of six pillars. The church was paved with marble and its walls partly faced with marble. Adjoining it is a chapel with a mosaic floor of geometric design. An inscription mentions the donors of the mosaic and the date. It was laid down in the 6th century "in the Episcopate of Thomas and under the Governorship of John". Beyond the chapel is the baptistry with its cruciform font, less well-preserved than the one in the South Church.

The recent restorations carried out by the Department for Landscaping and the Preservation of Historic Sites raise the curtain of history on the art, skills and pattern of life of an ancient people.

SOLOMON'S MINES

The Valley of Arabah, the rift that runs from the Dead Sea southwards to the Gulf of Aqaba, is one result of the prehistoric cataclasm that split the earth between the territories now known as Turkey and Africa. Another result is the exotic variety in the colour and configuration of the rocks that mark the "lips" of the cleft, standing at the base of the mountain ranges that rise on either side. What it would have taken a multitude of artistic hands to fashion in a multitude of lifetimes, nature committed in an instant. And what rough edges were left were polished by erosion. Of all the natural sculptures that abound in the area of the southern Arabah, none is more impressive than the two huge russet projections of rock that have been dubbed the "Pillars of Solomon".

Equally impressive is their setting. This must be literally one of the most colourful regions on earth. For the ancient eruption has spewed forth rocks, companions to the Pillars, with each exposed and mineral-encrusted stratum bearing the special colour of its ore. In the distance, the slopes of the Edom mountains in the east and of the plateau of Paran on the west are themselves bathed in rich reds and purples and blues as the light changes from sunrise to sunset. To complete this explosion of colour, the Red Sea has shot up a turquoise tongue of water, the Gulf of Aqaba, to meet the converging valley and blazing hills. Elath, at the head of the Gulf, lies sixteen miles south of the Pillars.

Modern Elath is close to the Biblical site encountered by the Israelites on their way to Canaan following their exodus from Egypt: "And when we passed . . . through the way of the plain from Elath, and from Ezion-gaber . . ." (Deuteronomy II, 8). This is also the area where king Solomon, in the middle of the 10th Century B.C., "made a navy of ships in Ezion-geber, which is beside Eloth, on the shore of the Red Sea, in the land of Edom." (I Kings IX, 26).* And it was certainly this part of the country that was being described in the Deuteronomy account of the Promised Land when the Israelites were told that, among its other virtues, it was "a land whose stones are iron, and out of whose hills thou mayest dig brass (copper)." (VIII, 9).

The meaning of this verse came boldly to life when the American archaeologist Dr. Nelson Glueck discovered and carried out an extensive excavation at the original site of Ezion-geber. He found that Solomon had done more than build a navy nearby. Solomon had also turned Ezion-geber into an industrial city, with huge smelters and workshops which produced the copper ingots and tools which he used both for his immense building programme and for his considerable export trade. The copper was bartered for gold and spices and other exotic

* The difference in spelling of these place-names in the Bible has been retained.

products from Africa, Arabia and India. The Bible mentions one such exchange with Ophir, noting that Solomon's ships "came to Ophir, and fetched from thence gold, four hundred and twenty talents, and brought it to king Solomon." In his facinating account of his remarkable discoveries, Glueck writes that "the elaborate copper smelter and manufacturing centre constructed by him (Solomon) at Ezion-geber is the largest that has thus far been discovered". The copper was not found at this spot. It was mined a few miles inland. The largest of the mining sites in the Arabah was the area of the Pillars. The name of the place is Timna. The raw ores were dug out of open mines and partly smelted in small stone furnaces. They were then transported to Ezion-geber where they were further refined and turned into ingots. At Timna, the waste slag was thrown aside and eventually formed large black mounds. Standing guard over king Solomon's mines at Timna were the two rock projections which are accordingly called the "Pillars of Solomon".

But if the Pillars "guarded" the mines, Solomon did not rely on nature to guard the army of slaves who worked the mines. These were the unfortunates who had been captured in battle. (This was the practice at the time, resorted to by both sides. Thus, while Edomite prisoners worked Solomon's mines, there were Judean prisoners slaving in the mines of Edom). To prevent their escape from their wretched labours, a strong wall was erected round the entire area of the mines and furnaces at Timna. Parts of this walled enclosure remain to this day.

Reconstructing the ancient smelting process, archaeologist Glueck showed that Solomon had anticipated by some three thousand years methods which revolutionised industry in the western world in the last century. Carefully located apertures in the walls of his smelting chambers opened into air channels skilfully sited to trap the constant north winds blowing down the Arabah funnel. These fanned the flames in the furnaces and kept them blazing at maximum heat all the time. As Glueck observes in his *Rivers in the Desert*, "No hand-bellows system was necessary, because with brilliant calculation, Solomon's engineers had harnessed the winds to furnish natural draught. The Bessemer principle of forced-air draught, discovered less than a century ago, was, in essence, already familiar three millennia back." Describing the huge smelter he had unearthed at Ezion-geber, designed on the same principle as the smaller ones at Timna, he says: "So well had the smelter been constructed, that when it had been completely exposed, we could place our hands on the flue-holes in the wall at the south end of the structure and feel the air emerging, which had entered through the flue-holes on the north side, a number of rooms away."

The mines, furnaces, slag heaps and ruins of Solomon's enclosure wall may be seen today. And visitors can carry home as a memento an authentic piece of slag discarded after smelting three thousand years ago. Nearby, closer to the main Elath road, stands modern Timna's large new copper mining plant, set up after the State of Israel came into being in 1948. Extraction of the ore is now mechanical, and output and quality are higher than they were in Solomon's time. But the very establishment of this plant is certainly due in part to the tradition started by the ancient Israelite king. As Dr. Glueck concluded from his archaeological research, Solomon was not only "a great ruler of legendary wisdom, and a highly successful merchant prince and shipping magnate, but . . . he was also a copper king of first rank, who transformed Israel into an industrial power."

CHRONOLOGICAL TABLE

PERIODS	CULTURAL FEATURES, EVENTS, AND LEADING PERSONALITIES	ARCHAELOGICAL SITES REFERRED TO IN THIS BOOK, WHERE REMAINS OF THE PERIOD HAVE BEEN FOUND
PALAEOLITHIC (Old Stone Age) Lower Palaeolithic 600 000 — 100 000 B.C.	Pebble culture (Primitive man) Hunting Hand axes First cave deposits	Ubediye (Jordan Valley) Mount Carmel caves
Middle Palaeolithic 100 000 — 50 000 B.C.	Galilee man	Wadi Amud Mount Carmel caves
Upper Palaeolithic 50 000 — 12 000 B.C.	Homo Sapiens	Mount Carmel caves
MESOLITHIC (Middle Stone Age) 12 000 — 7500 B.C.	Beginnings of agriculture Gathering of grain Hoes, picks, sickle-blades and stone mortars Beginnings of plastic art	
NEOLITHIC (New Stone Age) 7500—4000 B.C.	Yarmuk culture Permanent settlement Developed agricultural villages Domestication of animals Permanent shrines Fertility cults Beginnings of pottery towards end of period	Sha'ar Hagolan Tel Aviv area
CHALCOLITHIC (Copper Stone Age) 4000 — 3150 B.C.	Towns, villages Round and rectangular houses Underground dwellings Ghassulian culture Introduction of copper Well developed art — ivory, copper, stone, frescoes Secondary burials in house-shaped ossuaries	Lowest strata of Megiddo and Beth She'an Tel Aviv Azur Abu Ghosh Tell Gath Beersheba Caves of Bar Kochba Ein Gedi

BRONZE AGE			
Early Bronze 3150 — 2200 B.C.	Fortified towns Sanctuaries Cultural contacts with Egypt, Mesopotamia, Anatolia, Cyprus		Hazor Beth Yerach Beth She'an Megiddo Tell Gath Lachish

Middle Bronze
2200 — 1500 B.C.
	Execration Texts
	Age of the Patriarchs — Abraham,
	   Isaac, Jacob
	Political and cultural ties with
	   Egypt
	Hyksos invasion and domination
	   of Canaan and Egypt
	Beginnings of pictographic
	   alphabet
	Ceramic and metal industries
			Hazor
			Beth She'an
			Megiddo
			Jaffa
			Ashkelon
			Lachish

Late Bronze
1500 — 1200 B.C.
	Egyptian rule in Canaan with
	   vassal city-kingdoms
	Tell el-Amarna archives
	Exodus of the Israelites from
	   Egypt — Moses
	The Ten Commandments
	Conquest of Canaan by Israelite
	   tribes — Joshua
	Flourishing international trade
	Alphabetic writing
			Hazor
			Beth She'an
			Megiddo
			Jaffa
			Ashkelon
			Lachish

IRON AGE I
1200 — 922 B.C.
	Invasion of the "Sea Peoples" —
	   including the Philistines
	Settlement of Israelite tribes in
	   Canaan
	Period of the Judges — notably
	   Ehud, Deborah, Gideon,
	   Jephtha, Samson
	Philistine city-states
	Samuel
	United Monarchy (Saul, David,
	   Solomon) 1020—922
	David makes Jerusalem capital of
	   Israel
	Solomon builds Temple, and
	   guides Israel to peak of political,
	   economic and cultural prosperity
	Ties with Phoenicia
			Hazor
			Ein Gev
			Beth She'an
			Megiddo
			Tel Aviv (Tell Kasile)
			Azur
			Jerusalem
			Ramat Rachel
			Lachish
			Ein Gedi
			Solomon's mines

IRON AGE II 922 — 587 B.C.	*Divided Monarchy: kingdoms of Israel (922—722) and Judah (922—587) The prophets Elijah, Elisha, Amos, Hosea, I Isaiah (Chapters 1—39) and Micah Fall of Samaria, 722 The prophets Jeremiah, Zephaniah, Nahum, Habakkuk First deportation to Babylon, 597 The prophet Ezekiel Destruction of Jerusalem and of the First Temple, 587 Second deportation to Babylon, 587	Hazor Ein Gev Megiddo Tel Aviv (Tell Kasile) Jerusalem Ramat Rachel Lachish Ein Gedi Solomon's mines
PERSIAN PERIOD 587 — 332 B.C.	Babylonian captivity, 587—536 The prophet II Isaiah (Chapters 40—66) Edict by Cyrus granting Jews the right to return, 538 Return of the Jews from Babylon Zerubbabel, governor The prophets Haggai and Zechariah Building of the Second Temple (completed about 516) and walls of Jerusalem The prophets Obadiah and Malachi Judea an autonomous province of Persian empire Ezra and Nehemiah	Hazor Tel Aviv (Tell Kasile) Ramat Rachel Ashkelon Lachish Ein Gedi
HELLENISTIC PERIOD 332 — 63 B.C.	Hellenistic domination of the country with the conquest of the Persian empire by Alexander of Macedonia (Alexander the Great) in 332. Rule of the Ptolemies, 312—198 The Septuagint Rule of the Seleucids, 198—167 Maccabean War of Liberation, 167—141 (Mattathias and his sons, Judah the Maccabee (166—160), Jonathan (160—143), Simon (143—135), Eleazar and Johanan)	Beth Yerach Acre Jewish tombs in Jerusalem Ramat Rachel Ashkelon Mareshah Ein Gedi

---

* Names and dates of the 19 kings of Israel and the 20 kings of Judah are given in a separate table.

Rededication of Temple, 164/5
Hasmonean Dynasty (The
  Maccabees), 141—63 (and,
  partially, up to 37): John Hyrcanus
  (135—104), Judah Aristobulus
  (104—103), Alexander Jannai
  (103—76), Salome Alexandra
  (76—67), Aristobulus II (67—63).
  High Priest Hyrcanus was nominal
  ruler under the Romans after 63,
  and Jewish freedom was briefly
  regained under Mattathias
  Antigonus (40—37).
Pompey's conquest (63) and
  beginning of Roman rule
The Sages Hillel and Shammai

ROMAN PERIOD
63 B.C. — 324 A.D.

Hellenistic-Roman culture
Herodian Dynasty,
  37 B.C.—70A.D. (Herod the
  Great, 37 B.C.—4 B.C.)
Pontius Pilate, Roman Procurator
Jesus and the beginnings of
  Christianity
First Jewish war against the
  Romans, 66—73 A.D.
Fall of Jerusalem and destruction of
  the Second Temple, 70 A.D.
Epic of Massada, 73 A.D.
Jewish religious centre at Yavne—
  Rabbi Yohanan Ben Zakkai
Second Jewish war against the
  Romans, led by Bar Kochba,
  132—135 A.D.
Rabbi Akiva
Emperor Hadrian changes name of
  country from Judea to Syria
  Palestina (Palestine)
Bar Kochba documents
Completion of the Mishnah —
  Rabbi Yehudah Ha'Nasi
Roman theatres
Early synagogues

Galilean synagogues
  of Capernaum,
  Bar'am and Khorazin
Beth She'an
Beth She'arim
Caesarea
Jerusalem
Ramat Rachel
Ashkelon
Avdat
Shivta
Massada
Caves of Bar Kochba

BYZANTINE PERIOD
324 — 640 A.D.

Palestine part of Byzantine empire
Building of synagogues
Completion of "Jerusalem"
  Talmud

Synagogues of Beth
  Yerach, Hammath
  (Tiberias), Beth She'an,
  Beth Alpha, Caesarea.

	Building of churches Well developed mosaic art Persian conquest, 614 Re-conquest by Byzantium, 627 Beginning of Moslem conquest, 634	Churches and monasteries at Beth Yerach, Beth She'an, Beth She'arim, Caesarea, Abu Ghosh, Jerusalem, Ramat Rachel, Avdat, Shivta.
MOSLEM PERIOD 640 — 1099 A.D.	Palestine becomes an unimportant province of the Moslem empire Decline and impoverishment of the country	Minya Tell Kasile Ramla Jerusalem Ashkelon
CRUSADER PERIOD 1099 — 1291 A.D.	Development and fortification of coastal cities Building of castles Feudal agriculture in Crusader estates Rabbi Moses Ben Maimon (The Rambam, Maimonides)	Safad Horns of Hattin Belvoir Acre Mount Tabor Montfort Yehiam Athlit Caesarea Ramla Lod Abu Ghosh Jerusalem Ashkelon Mareshah Beth Govrin
MAMELUKE PERIOD 1291 — 1517 A.D.	Systematic destruction of coastal cities Economic decline Neglect of land	Tell Kasile Jaffa Ramla Lod
TURKISH PERIOD 1517 — 1917 A.D.		Minya Tiberias Safad Acre Jaffa Abu Ghosh Ashkelon

THE HEBREW MONARCHIES

UNITED MONARCHY

Saul	about 1020—1000 B.C.
David	about 1000—961
Solomon	about 961—922

DIVIDED MONARCHY

KINGDOM OF JUDAH, 922—587 B.C.			KINGDOM OF ISRAEL, 922—722 B.C	
Prophets				*Prophets*
	Rehoboam, 922—915		Jeroboam, 922—901	
	Abijam, 915—913		Nadab, 901—900	
	Asa, 913—873		Baasha, 900—877	
	Jehoshaphat, 873—849		Elah, 877—876	
			Zimri, 876	
			Omri, 876—869	
			Ahab, 869—850	Elijah
	Jehoram, 849—842		Ahaziah, 850—849	
	Ahaziah, 842		Jehoram, 849—842	Elisha
	Athaliah, 842—837		Jehu, 842—815	
	Joash, 837—800		Jehoahaz, 815—801	
	Amaziah, 800—783		Jehoash, 801—786	
	Uzziah, 783—742		Jeroboam II, 786—746	Amos
			Zechariah, 746—745	Hosea
			Shallum, 745	
Isaiah	Jotham, 742—735		Menahem, 745—738	
Micah			Pekahiah, 738—737	
	Ahaz, 735—715		Pekah, 737—732	
			Hoshea, 732—724	
	Hezekiah, 715—687		(Fall of Samaria, 722)	
	Manasseh, 687—642			
	Amon, 642—640			
Jeremiah	Josiah, 640—609			
Zephaniah	Jehoahaz, 609			
Nahum				
Habakkuk	Jehoiakim, 609—598			
	Jehoiachin, 598—597			
Ezekiel	Zedekiah, 597—587			
	(Fall of Jerusalem, 587)			

(NOTE: Scholars differ over the dating of several of the periods of the Hebrew monarchies. The range of difference in some cases is more than a decade, in others only two or three years. We have followed the chronology of the greatest living Biblical archaeologist, W.F. Albright.)

SELECTED BIBLIOGRAPHY

GENERAL

F.M. Abel, *Géographie de la Palestine, I ,II. Paris, 1932, 1938.*
　　Histoire de la Palestine, depuis la conquête d'Alexandre jusqu'a l'invasion Arabe, I, II. Paris, 1952.
W.F. Albright, *The Archaeology of Palestine. New York (Penguin Books), 1949.*
　　From the Stone Age to Christianity. New York, 1957.
M. Avi-Yonah, *Historical Geography of Palestine, 3rd Ed., Jerusalem, 1963.*
I. Ben-Zvi, *Eretz-Yisrael under Ottoman Rule.* (Hebrew) *Jerusalem, 1955.*
J. Bright, *A History of Israel. New York, 1960.*
C.R. Conder and H.H. Kitchener, *The Survey of Western Palestine, I, II, III. London, 1881–83.*
E.R. Goodenough, *Jewish Symbols in the Greco-Roman Period, I. New York, 1953.*
C. Enlart, *Les Monuments des Croisés dans le Royaume de Jerusalem, II. Paris, 1928.*
Josephus Flavius, *The Wars of the Jews with the Romans.*
H. Kohl and C. Watzinger, *Antike Synagogen in Galilaea. Leipzig, 1916.*
G. Le Strange, *Palestine under the Moslems. London, 1890.*
S.A.B. Mercer, *The Tell El-Amarna Tablets, I, II. Toronto, 1939.*
J. Parkes, *A History of Palestine from 135 A.D. to Modern Times. London, 1949.*
G. Posner, *Princes et pays d'Asie de Nubie. Brussels, 1940.* (For material on the Execration Texts.)
J. Prawer, *A History of the Latin Kingdoms of Jerusalem, I, II.* (Hebrew) *Jerusalem, 1963.*
I. Press, *Encyclopaedia of Eretz-Yisrael, I, II, III, IV.* (Hebrew) *Jerusalem, 1946–55.*
J.B. Pritchard, ed., *Ancient Near Eastern Texts. Oxford, 1950.*
C. Roth, *Short History of the Jewish People. London, 1948.*
S. Runciman, *A History of the Crusades, I, II, III. London, 1951–55.*
George Adam Smith, *The Historical Geography of the Holy Land. London, 1894 (1st Ed.)*
E.L. Sukenik, *Ancient Synagogues in Palestine and Greece. London, 1934.*
P. Thomsen, *Loca Sancta. Halle, 1907.*
T. Wright, ed., *Early Travels in Palestine. London, 1848.*
G.E. Wright and F.V. Filson, *The Westminster Historical Atlas to the Bible. Philadelphia, 1946.*
Y. Yadin, *The Art of Warfare in Biblical Lands. New York, 1963.*
S. Yeivin and C.Z. Hirshberg, eds., *Eretz Kinnaroth.* (Hebrew) *Jerusalem, 1950.*

[In the following bibliography for the individual sites, some books which already appear in the general list are mentioned again where they contain special material on a particular site. In such cases, they are listed first, and are referred to by author alone.]

JERUSALEM

Press, *vols. II and III.*
N. Avigad, *Ancient Monuments in the Kidron Valley. Jerusalem, 1954.*
M. Avi-Yonah, ed., *The Book of Jerusalem, I.* (From its origins up to the destruction of the Second Temple.) (Hebrew) *Jerusalem, 1956.*
H. Kendall, *Jerusalem, The City Plan — Preservation and Development during the British Mandate, 1918–48. London, 1948.*
L.A. Mayer and M. Avi-Yonah, *Concise Bibliography of Excavations in Palestine — Jerusalem. QDAP I, 1932.*
B. Mazar *in Encyclopaedia Biblica III.* (Hebrew) *Jerusalem, 1958.*
J. Simons, *Jerusalem in the Old Testament. Leiden, 1952.*
George Adam Smith, *Jerusalem from the Earliest Times to A.D. 70, I, II. London, 1907–8.*
E.L. Sukenik and L.A. Mayer, *The Third Wall of Jerusalem. Jerusalem, 1930.*

BAR'AM

Goodenough; Khol and Watzinger; Sukenik.

HAZOR

J. Garstang, *The Site of Hazor. Annals of Archaeology and Anthropology XIV. 1927.*
Y. Yadin, Y. Aharoni, Ruth Amiram, Trude Dothan, I. Dunayevsky, J. Perrot: *Hazor I, An Account of the First Season of Excavations, 1955. Jerusalem, 1958.*
　　Hazor II is an account of the Second Season, 1956. Jerusalem, 1960.
　　Hazor III and IV, Jerusalem, 1961, contain only the plates of the finds during the third and fourth seasons. The acounts were not yet published when this book went to press.
Olga Tufnell, *Hazor, Samaria and Lachish. PEQ 91, 1959.*

SAFAD

Conder and Kitchener *vol. I*; Press, *vol. IV*.
I. Ben Zvi, *The Jewish fortress of the 16th Century . . . in Safad*. (Hebrew) BJPES X, 1943.
J. Braslavski, *Geniza Fragments referring to Safad*. (Hebrew) BJPES IX, 1942.
E.W.G. Masterman, *Safed*. PEFQst 46, 1914.

MERON

Abel, *(Géographie), vol. II;* Goodenough; Kohl and Watzinger; Press, *vol. III*.
Y. Aharoni, *The Tribes of Israel in Upper Galilee*. (Hebrew) Jerusalem, 1956.

SEA OF GALILEE

Abel, *(Géographie), vol. I; Eretz Kinnaroth, particularly the contributions of* D. Amiran, M. Stekelis S. Yeivin,
    E.L. Sukenik and Y. Weitz.
J.G. Duncan, *The Sea of Tiberias and its Environs*. PEFQst 58, 1926.
A. Frei, *Beobachten vom See Genezareth*. ZDPV IX, 1886.
R. de Haas, *"Galilee", a Historical and Geographical Description of Lake Galilee and Surroundings*. Jerusalem, 1933.

KHORAZIN

Goodenough; Kohl and Watzinger; Sukenik.

MINYA

O. Grabar, J. Perrot, B. Ravani et Myriam Rosen: *Sondages à Khirbet el-Minyeh*. IEJ 10, 1960.
A.M. Schneider, *Hirbet El-Minje am See Genesareth. Les Annales Archéologiques de Syrie*, II, 1952.

WADI-AMUD

F. Turville-Peter, *Researches in Prehistoric Galilee 1925–6. (With Sections by D.M. Bate and C. Baynes, and a
    Report on the Galilee Skull by A. Keith.)* London, 1927.

ARBEL

Abel, *(Géographie), vol. II;* Goodenough; Kohl and Watzinger; Press, *vol. I*.

SHA'AR HAGOLAN

M. Stekelis, *A New Neolithic Industry: The Yarmukian of Palestine*. IEJ 1, 1950–51.

EIN GEV

[B. Mazar's report of the Ein Gev excavations had not yet been published when this book went to press.]

SUSSITA

Abel, *(Géographie), vol. II;* Press, *vol. III*.

CAPERNAUM

Goodenough; Kohl and Watzinger; Sukenik.
G. Orfali, *Capharnaum et ses Ruines*. Paris, 1922.

TABGHA

A.M. Schneider, *The Church of the Multiplying of the Loaves and Fishes at Tabgha on the Lake of Gennesaret and
    its Mosaics*. London, 1937.

MOUNT OF THE BEATITUDES

J.G. Duncan, *Mount of the Beatitudes*. PEFQst 58, 1926.
P.B. Bagatti, *La Cappella sul monte della Beatudini. Rivista Di Archeologia Cristiana*, XIV, 1937.

TIBERIAS

Abel, (*Géographie*), *vol. II; Eretz Kinnaroth, particularly the contributions of* G. Landau, M. Schwabe, B. Klar,
 J. Barslavsky and Y.M. Toledano.
M. Avi-Yonah, *The Foundation of Tiberias. IEJ 1, 1950.*
S. Kindler, *The Coins of Tiberias. Tiberias, 1961.*
N. Slousch, *The Excavations at Tiberias.* (Hebrew) *BJPES I, 1921.*
L.H. Vincent, *Les Fouilles juives d'El Hammam à Tibériade. RB 30, 1921, and RB 31, 1922.*

BETH YERACH

P. Bar-Adon, *Sinabra and Beth Yerach in the light of the Sources and Archaeological Finds.* (Hebrew) *EI IV, 1956.*
P. Delougaz and R.C. Haines, *A Byzantine Church at Khirbet al-Karak. Chicago, 1960.*
B. Maisler (Mazar), M. Stekelis and M. Avi-Yonah: *The Excavations at Beth Yerach (Khirbet el-Kerak) 1944–46.*
 IEJ 2, 1952.

MOUNT TABOR

Abel, (*Géographie*), *vol. I;* Conder and Kitchener, *vol. I;* Press, *vol. II.*
B. Meisterman, *Le Mont Thabor. Paris, 1900.*

NAZARETH

E. Blyth, *Nazareth, A Forgotten Page in English History. PEFQst 52, 1920.*
C. Kopp, *Beiträge zur Geschichte Nazareths. JPOS XVIII, 1938; XIX, 1939/40; XX, 1946; and XXI, 1948.*
G. Schumacher, *Das jetzige Nazareth. ZDPV XIII, 1890.*
P. Viaud, *Nazareth et ses deux églises de l'annonciation et de St. Joseph d'apres les fouilles récent es. Paris, 1910.*

BETH SHE'AN

Conder and Kitchener, *vol. II.*
S. Applebaum, *The Roman Theatre of Beth She'an. BIES XXV, 1961.*
M. Avi-Yonah, *Mosaic pavements at El Hammam, Beisan. QDAP V, 1936.*
 A Jewish Relief from Beth She'an. BJPES VIII, 1940.
 Scythopolis. IEJ 12, 1962.
A. Rowe, *The Topography and History of Beth Shan, I. Philadelphia, 1930.*
 The Four Canaanite Temples of Beth Shan, II, Part I. 1940.
G.M. Fitzgerald, *The Four Canaanite Temples of Beth Shan, II, Part II.*
 Beth Shan Excavations 1921–23, III: The Arab and Byzantine Levels. 1931.
 A Sixth Century Monastery at Beth Shan, IV. 1939.
B. Maisler (Mazar), *The Chronology of the Beth She'an Temples. BIES XVI, 1951.*
Three contributions to "The Beth She'an Valley" (Hebrew) *Jerusalem, 1962:*
 B. Mazar: *The Valley of Beth She'an in Biblical Times.*
 S. Yeivin: *Beth She'an and its Temples in the period of Egyptian Rule.*
 R. Amiram: *The Tell of Beth She'an.*

BETH ALPHA

Goodenough; Sukenik.
N. Avigad, *The mosaic pavement of the Beth Alpha synagogue and its place in the history of Jewish art.* (Hebrew)
 Contributed to "The Beth She'an valley", Jerusalem, 1962.
E.L. Sukenik, *The Ancient Synagogue of Beth Alpha. Jerusalem, 1932.*

BETH SHE'ARIM

B. Mazar (Maisler), *Beth She'arim, Report on the Excavations during 1936–40, I.* (Hebrew) *Jerusalem, 1957.*
 (2nd Ed.)
 The Eighth Season of Excavations at Beth She'arim, 1956. (Hebrew) *BIES, 1957.*
N. Avigad, *Excavations at Beth She'arim, 1953, 54, 55, 58. IEJ 4, 1954; 5, 1955; 7, 1957; and 9, 1959.*

MEGIDDO

P.L.O. Guy and R.M. Engberg, *Megiddo Tombs. Chicago, 1938.*
R.S. Lamon, *The Megiddo Water System. Chicago, 1935.*
R.S. Lamon and G.M. Shipton, *Megiddo I, Seasons of 1925–34. Chicago, 1939.*

G. Loud, *Megiddo II, Seasons of 1935–39. Chicago, 1948.*
    The Megiddo Ivories. Chicago, 1939.
G. Schumacher, *Tell El-Mutesellim I (Fundebricht). Leipzig, 1908.*
C. Watzinger, *Tell El-Mutesellim II (Die Funde). Leipzig, 1929.*
Y. Yadin, *New light on Solomon's Megiddo. Biblical Archaeologist XXIII, 1960.*
    Hazor, Gezer and Megiddo in Solomon's times. (Hebrew) Contributed to "*In the days of the First Temple*",
    ed. by A. Malamat. *Jerusalem, 1961.*

MONTFORT

Conder and Kitchener, *vol. I;* Prawer; Runciman, *vol. III.*
B. Dean, *A Crusaders' Fortress in Palestine. Bulletin of the Metropolitan Museum of Art, September 1927.*
E.W.G. Masterman, *A Crusaders' Fortress in Palestine. PEFQst 60, 1928.*

ACRE

Abel, *(Géographei), vol. II;* Conder and Kitchener, *vol. I;* Enlart, *vol. II;* Prawer; Press, *vol. IV;* Runciman,
    vols. II and III.
R.G. Alderson, *Notes on Acre and some of the coast defences of Syria. London, 1844.*
C.N. Johns and M. Makhouly, *Guide to Acre. Jerusalem, 1946.* (2nd Ed.)
Department for Landscaping and the Preservation of Historic Sites: *Acre, the Old City; Survey and Planning.*
    Jerusalem, 1963.

HAIFA

L. Oliphant, *Haifa, or Life in Modern Palestine. Edinburgh, 1887.*
L. Schatner, *Haifa, a study in the relation of city and coast. IEJ 4, 1954.*
Z. Vilnay, *Haifa, Past and Future.* (Hebrew) *Tel Aviv, 1936.*

Carmel

M. Avi-Yonah, *Mount Carmel and the god of Baalbek. IEJ 2, 1951.*
Dorothy A.E. Garrod, *The Stone Age of Mount Carmel, I. Oxford, 1937.*
Th. D. McCown and A. Keith, *The Stone Age of Mount Carmel, II. Oxford, 1939.*
E. v Mulinen, *Beiträge zur Kenntnis des Karmels. ZDPV 30 and 31, 1907 and 1908.*
M. Stekelis and Tamar Yizraeli, *Excavations at Nahal Oren (Preliminary Report). IEJ 13, 1963.*
E. Wreschner, *Prehistoric Survey of the Carmel (Preliminary Report).* (Hebrew). Contributed to "*Mitekufat Ha'even*",
    II. Jerusalem, 1961.

ATHLIT

Conder and Kitchener, *vol. I;* Enlart, *vol. II.*
R. Fedden and J. Thomson, *Crusader Castles. London, 1957.*
C.N. Johns, *Excavations at Pilgrims' Castle (Atlit). QDAP I, 1931; II, 1933; III, 1934; IV, 1935; V, 1936;*
    and VI, 1938.

CAESAREA

M. Avi-Yonah, *The Synagogue of Caesarea, Preliminary Report. Bulletin III of the L.M. Rabinowitz Fund for the*
    Exploration of Ancient Synagogues, 1960.
    A list of Priestly Courses from Caesarea. IEJ 12, 1962.
L. Haefeli, *Caesarea am Meer. Munster, 1923.*
H. Hamburger, *Caesarea coin finds and the history of the city.* (Hebrew) *BIES XV, 1950.*
L. Kadman, *The Coins of Caesarea Maritima. Jerusalem, 1957.*
A. Reifenberg, *Caesarea: A Study in the Decline of a Town. IEJ I, 1950–51.*
S. Yeivin, *Excavations at Caesarea Maritima. Archaeology (U.S.A.) 8, 1955.*

TEL AVIV-JAFFA

F.M. Abel, *Jaffa au Moyen-Age. JPOS XX, 1946.*
M. Broshi in *Encyclopaedia Biblica III.* (Hebrew) *Jerusalem, 1958.*
C. Clermont-Ganneau, *Archaeological Researches in Palestine 1873–1874. London, 1896.*
Y. Kaplan, *The Archaeology and History of Tel Aviv-Jaffa.* (Hebrew) *Tel Aviv, 1959.*
B. Maisler (Mazar), *The Excavations at Tell Qasile, Preliminary Report. IEJ I, 1950–51.*
S. Tolkowski, *The Gateway of Palestine; a History of Jaffa. London, 1924.*
    The Destruction of the Jewish Navy at Jaffa in the year 68 A.D. PEFQst 60, 1928.

RAMLA

Conder and Kitchener, *vol. II*; Enlart, *vol. II*; Press, *vol. IV*.
S. Assaf, *Documents relating to the Jewish communities in Ramla and the Shephela.* (Hebrew) BJPES VIII, 1941.
Y. Kaplan, *Excavations at the White Mosque in Ramla. Atiqot II, Jerusalem, 1959.*
L.A. Mayer, *Muslim Religious Buildings in Israel. Jerusalem, 1950.*

LOD (Lydda)

Abel, (*Geographie*), *vol. II*; Conder and Kitchener, *vol. II*; Press, *vol. III*.
C. Clermont-Ganneau, *Archaeological Researches in Palestine 1873–1874. London, 1896.*
Z. Kallai *in Encyclopaedia Biblica IV.* (Hebrew) Jerusalem, 1962.
L.A. Mayer, *Muslim Religious Buildings in Israel. Jerusalem, 1950.*

ABU GHOSH

R. de Vaux and A.M. Steve, *Fouilles à Qaryet El-Enab, Abu Gosh, Palestine. Paris, 1950.*
J. Perrot, *Le Néolithique d'Abou Gosh. Syria XXIX, 1952.*

ASHKELON

Conder and Kitchener, *vol. III*.
U. Ben Horin, *Lady Hester Stanhope's excavations at Ashkelon in 1815.* (Hebrew) BJPES XII, 1945–46.
J. Garstang, *The Excavations at Askalon. PEFQst 53, 1921; 54, 1922; and 56, 1924.*
D. Mackenzie, *The Philistine City of Askelon. PEFQst 45, 1913.*
W.J. Phytian-Adams, *History of Ascalon. PEFQst 53, 1921.*

LACHISH

N. Avigad and H. Tur-Sinai *in Encyclopaedia Biblica IV.* (Hebrew) Jerusalem, 1962.
H. Torczyner (Tur-Sinai) and others. *Lachish I, The Lachish Letters. London, 1938.*
   The Lachish Ostraca. (Hebrew) Jerusalem, 1940.
Olga Tufnell and others, *Lachish II, The Fosse Temple. London, 1940.*
   Lachish III, The Iron Age. London, 1953.
   Lachish IV, The Bronze Age. London, 1958.

MARESHAH AND BETH GOVRIN

F.M. Abel, *Découvertes récentes à Beit-Djebrin. RB 33, 1924.*
F.J. Bliss and R.A.S. Macalister, *Excavations in Palestine 1898–1900. London, 1902.*
C. Clermont-Ganneau, *Archaeological Researches in Palestine 1873–1874. London, 1896.*
J.B. Peters and H. Thiersch, *Painted Tombs in the Necropolis of Mariss (Mareshah). London, 1905.*
E.L. Sukenik, *A Synagogue Inscription from Beit Jibrin. JPOS X, 1930.*

BEERSHEBA

M. Dothan, *Excavations at Horvat Beter (Beersheba). Atiqot II, 1959.*
S. Hillelson, *Notes on the Tribes of Beersheba District. PEQ 69, 1937 and PEQ 70, 1938.*
J. Perrot, *The Excavations at Tell Abu Matar near Beersheba. IEJ 5, 1955.*
   The Dawn of History in Southern Palestine. Archaeology (U.S.A.) 12, 1959.
   Statuettes en ivoire et autres objets en ivoire et en as provenant de gisements préhistoriques de la région de Beershéba. Syria XXXVI, 1959.

MASSADA

M. Avi-Yonah, N. Avigad, Y. Aharoni, I. Dunayevsky, S. Guttman: *Massada, Survey and Excavations 1955–56 Jerusalem, 1957. (Also in IEJ 7, 1957).*
Josephus, *Wars of the Jews.*
A. Schulten, *Massada. ZDPV 56, 1933.*

CAVES OF BAR KOCHBA

Y. Aharoni, *The Caves of Nahal Hever. Atiqot III, 1961.*
N. Avigad, Y. Aharoni, P. Bar-Adon, Y. Yadin and others: *Judean Desert Caves: Survey and Excavations 1960. Jerusalem, 1961. (Also in IEJ 11, 1961).*
   Survey and Excavations 1961. Jerusalem, 1962. (Also in IEJ 12, 1962.)
Y. Yadin, *The Finds from the Bar Kochba Period in the "Cave of the Letters". Jerusalem, 1963.*

EIN GEDI

B. Mazar, Trude Dothan and I. Dunayevsky, *Ein Gedi, Archaeological Excavations 1961–62. (Hebrew) BIES XXII, Jerusalem, 1963. [English edition to be published shortly.]*

AVDAT

M. Avi-Yonah and A. Negev, *A City of the Negeb, Excavations in Nabatean, Roman and Byzantine Eboda. Illustrated London News,* 26.11.1960.
N. Glueck, *Rivers in the Desert. New York, 1959.*
A. Negev, *Avdat, a Caravan Halt in the Negev. Archaeology (U.S.A.) 14, 1961.*
Nabatean Inscriptions from Avdat (Oboda), I and II. IEJ 11, 1960 and IEJ 13, 1962.
C.L. Woolley and T.E. Lawrence, *The Wilderness of Zin. PEFA III, 1914–15.*

SHIVTA

N. Glueck, *Rivers in the Desert. New York, 1959.*
Y. Kedar, *Ancient Agriculture at Shivta in the Negev. IEJ 7, 1957.*
C.L. Woolley and T.E. Lawrence, *The Wilderness of Zin. PEFA III, 1914–15.*

SOLOMON'S MINES

N. Glueck, *The Excavations of Solomon's Seaport — Ezion Geber. The Smithsonian Report for 1941.*
Rivers in the Desert. New York 1959.
Elath and Ezion-Geber. (Hebrew) Address at Elath to the 18th Archaeological Convention, October 1962. Jerusalem, 1963.

ABBREVIATIONS

BIES — *Bulletin of the Israel Exploration Society. (Hebrew) Jerusalem*
BJPES — *Bulletin of the Jewish Palestine Exploration Society. (Hebrew) Jerusalem*
EI — *Eretz-Israel, archaeological, historical and geographical studies, published by the Israel Exploration Society. Jerusalem*
IEJ — *Israel Exploration Journal. Jerusalem*
JPOS — *Journal of the Palestine Oriental Society. Jerusalem*
PEFA — *Palestine Exploration Fund Annual. London*
PEFQst — *Palestine Exploration Fund, Quarterly Statement. London*
PEQ — *Palestine Exploration Quarterly. London*
QDAP — *Quarterly of the Department of Antiquities in Palestine. Jerusalem*
RB — *Revue Biblique. Jerusalem and Paris*
ZDPV — *Zeitschrift des Deutschen Palästina-Vereins. Leipzig*

INDEX

Many of the illustrations in this volume are
reproduced by courtesy of
The Oriental Institute, University of Chicago
Israel Government Department for Landscaping
  and Preservation of Historic Sites
Israel Government Department of Antiquities
Israel Government Press Office
Israel Government Tourist Corporation
The Hebrew University, Jerusalem

Credits for the remaining photographs go to
A. Pratelli, Milano
I. Bochenek, Tel-Aviv
P. Csasznik, Jerusalem
E. Glass
P. Gross, Tel-Aviv
E. Ilani, Jerusalem
Mirlin-Yaron, Tel-Aviv
Israel Press Photographers Association
"Pri-Or", Tel-Aviv
J. Schweig, Jerusalem
A. Volk, Jerusalem